THE LAST SELF-HELP BOOK

Before Getting Results

by
Jerome Lund

The Barclay Press
San Francisco, California

Published by The Barclay Press, San Francisco, California

TO MARCIA
WHO LIGHTS UP MY LIFE

ACKNOWLEDGEMENTS

This book could not have been written without the support of some very special people. First and foremost I wish to thank my parents, Grace and Harold, who live by the principles described in this book. In addition, I want to express my deepest gratitude for the support and knowledge of Dr. H. Frederick Vogt, Rev. Roger Teel, Dr. James Melton, Dr. John Lyke, and Peg Smiley, my longtime friend and mentor.

I needed and received a great deal of technical assistance from Christie Chester, Laveda Chadwick, Pat Windbigler, Dr. Ellen Tawson, and Doug Lyke, Without them, the task would have been insurmountable.

CONTENTS

PART ONE
THE THEORY

CHAPTER I
INTRODUCTION

This is a book about making changes in your life—significant, important, positive, startling changes. The only difference between this book and other self-help books you have read is that it gives you a step-by-step method for implementing the changes necessary to establish and realize your goals. The method is simple and time-tested, and will be spelled out so you can begin to use it immediately to feel the way you want to feel, and to have the things you want. The method will be presented clearly and concisely so you will know precisely what to do and when to do it.

The premise on which the method is based is not new. It has been drawn from several different sources, systematized, and used by hundreds of others to radically change their lives for the better. The premise is this: You have much more power available within yourself than you think you have, and you can use this power to change your life, regardless of your present situation. Not a new idea, to be sure; however, this book is going to show you how the power works and how you can begin using it now. The method will not be obscure, and will be explained simply and clearly so that you can begin putting it into practice immediately, thereby moving from where you are now to where you want to be. The method always works, and it works with amazing rapidity. With this in mind, let us begin.

First, we must take a moment to clarify an idea that may or may not cause you problems. This book will be mentioning spiritual principles from time to time. Spiritual principles have nothing to do with religion or religious principles. If the idea is foreign to you, or should you be athiestic or agnostic, do not worry. All that is asked is that you keep an open mind. If you can do that, you will come to the same conclusion in a different manner. And what is the conclusion? Simply that you and I have much more power available to us than we had imagined. The use of this power does not require any particular type of belief system, and it is amenable to all belief systems. In other words, do not be put off by semantics. You can believe in God, the great spirit, universal mind, or only in the power of yourself, and still effectively use these principles to change your life.

I might also add that I began using these principles in a quite different place from that in which I find myself today. I was broke, I was depressed, I was without friends, I was without much hope, and caught up in what I perceived to be the futility of life. All in all, my life was not going well. During this time I happened to come across several books which, in effect, explained to me that there was another way, a "truth" about life, and if I could only find it, everything would be fine. The trouble with those books, although chock-full of good ideas, was that they did not state in specific terms what this truth was; and although they alluded to the many wonderful things that I should be doing, none of them revealed how to do them. Thus, it was a long struggle to find these answers for myself. We are going to correct that policy right now. We are going to decide what this truth is and how to do the things we need to do to make positive changes in our lives.

The truth is this: There is a power in you right now, and when used properly will allow you to feel the way you want to feel, and allow you to have the kind of life you want to have. And this is how it works: Whatever is going on in your mind right now will be produced in your life tomorrow. You can, through a systematic process, change what you are thinking in such a way as to lead to the results you want. You may have heard this before. The only thing different about this book is the systematic, step-by-step approach that will give you practical tools to use the principles we are going to discuss, and which will result in the desired changes in your life.

Most of us feel we are a product of our environment.

We look at the world around us and the circumstances in which we find ourselves, and come to the conclusion our lives are the result of our cicumstances. We take into consideration the economic situation, hear and see the "signs of the times", and attempt to modify our environment or circumstances accordingly. Now, if we are to take the position that the truth of the matter is that thoughts become things, that what is going on in our heads is going on in our lives, a significant thing can and will happen. We will stop trying to adjust to circumstances which we feel are beyond our control, and we will in fact be able to immediately rise above any circumstances in which we find ourselves. If you will take a little time to think about your life you will begin to see a pattern. You will see, if you look closely and honestly, that everything that has happened to you, all of your successes, all of your failures, large or small, were precipitated by a system of thought. Certain beliefs were present preceding any event in your life that could have led to no other result. When you received an A on an examination, or when you obtained a position of employment, you believed that was going to be the end result of your efforts, and the activity necessary to produce that result followed.

The tendency will be to argue with the above statement, saying, perhaps, that you really did not know whether you were going to pass or fail the exam or the employment interview and were quite surprised about the outcome. However, you are probably talking about what you felt, not what you believed. These are two important ideas. The way you feel does not necessarily coincide with what you believe. When you begin to work towards a goal, preparing for an exam or an employment interview, for instance, your belief is that you have a good chance of successfully realizing your goal. Fears, doubts, uncertainties, are feelings about the outcome. And if the negative feelings do not overcome and substitute for the basic belief, then the result will be according to what you believe the outcome ought to be. Therefore, when we say thoughts become things, we are saying that what you believe is going to happen will happen, even if from time to time it feels as if you believe something different. This is not to say that feelings are unimportant. It is simply saying that your beliefs, and not your feelings about those beliefs, are what produce the results in your life and have always been producing the results you have been experiencing.

A good example of the above is given by Fredric Bailes in his book, Hidden Power for Human Problems. Dr. Bailes spent most of his life in the city. He and his wife purchased a cabin in the mountains, and in the spring Dr. Bailes planted flower seeds in the front lawn. When he had completed this task, he told his wife that he really could not believe that flowers would result from putting those seeds in the ground. His wife corrected him saying that he was feeling doubt that the flowers would grow, but he actually believed they would. The fact that he planted the seeds, gave them fertilizer, and intended to weed and water them were all actions precipitated by a belief system that the flowers would be produced in due time. If the feelings of doubt had been the primary belief system, he would have not planted the seeds in the first place; of course before very long the Bailes had a front lawn overflowing with flowers.

The point here is that often we are thinking one thing, believing another, and feeling a third. Only the thoughts that coincide with what we really believe are the thoughts that produce results in our lives. When we are looking back through our lives in an attempt to prove that everything that happened to us was preceded by a system of thought, we must look closely to see what our basic beliefs about the situation were at the time. All in all, we should be able to determine that our thinking led to certain activity and feelings which could not have resulted in any other thing happening than that which did happen, no matter what the circumstances were at the time, because the circumstances from beginning to end always affect us according to what we are thinking and believing at the time. In fact, the circumstances arise out of our belief systems.

Now, if the circumstances in our lives are results of what we have been thinking; or at the very least, are significantly impacted by our beliefs surrounding them, then the way to make changes is to change our thinking and beliefs, and the circumstances will automatically change. This is the basic premise upon which this entire philosophy rests.

The primary problem arises from the fact that most

of us are seldom thinking about the things we want, rather we spend most of our day thinking about what we do not want. We begin our day complaining to ourselves about the weather, the poor state of our health, the problems we will face at work, and of course, the traffic on the freeway. We see ourselves as proceeding into the world to attempt to deal with the circumstances of our lives, feeling those circumstances control us. At coffee break we sit down to discuss the ills of the world, the company, and our families and friends. We discuss crime, war, economic ruin, poor management, health, incompetency, and a dozen other things we hope will never catch up with us. However, we get the feeling that we are only one step ahead of all of these calamities. By the time we have struggled home through the traffic or on the crowded bus with everyone a potential enemy, if not a potential killer, and have gone through the evening thinking and discussing all the unfairness, backbiting, and again the incompetency of our colleagues at work, we finally settle down to the late evening news where we can see the crime, pestilence, corruption, sickness and war in living color. Little wonder then, if thoughts become things in our lives, that our lives are not going as well as they should. Some of us by way of compensation, exercise, run, read positive books, or join self-help groups. However, for most of us, our daily dose of positive thinking does not in any way equal the amount of time spent in random or negative thinking.

The questions then arise: How can we change this

type of thinking, and why should we change it? How do we know that thoughts become things? These ideas do not seem to coincide with what we have experienced to date. How can we have what we want just by thinking the right thoughts, particularly when we are surrounded by what appear to be uncontrollable and powerful circumstances? These are real concerns, particularly if we have been doing our best to think and act constructively, and in spite of this our plans seem to go awry. The thing we need to know, it would appear, is whether or not our belief systems are demonstrating in our lives. What is the theory that underlies this principle, and how can we apply it in our lives so that the end result is that we get what we want?

We will answer these questions by first discussing the theoretical basis for the ideas so far expressed; then we will explore precisely how to apply them in a systematic, consistent manner so that we end up exactly where we want to be.

CHAPTER II
THE MIND, THE BRAIN, AND THE PHYSICAL WORLD

Your brain is the most magnificent mechanism on earth. It is more complex in structure than the most sophisticated computer that our scientists could imagine in their wildest dreams. It has well over 20 billion cells or neurons, each capable of assimilating, storing, and organizing infinite amounts of material. Your brain controls an equally magnificent organ—your body. It keeps everything working in harmony and balance. Your brain and your body are designed to allow you to operate successfully within your environment.

Your mind, on the other hand, is the thing that is in control of your brain. Discussion of what the mind is—that thing behind the operation of the brain—has been going on for centuries. For our purposes, your mind is that thinking, conscious part of you that is really you. The brain is the computer, so to speak, and the mind is the computer operator. We have here a hierarchy of systems, with the mind at the top, then the brain, the body, and finally the external world of your affairs.

The system that is you operates in somewhat the following manner:

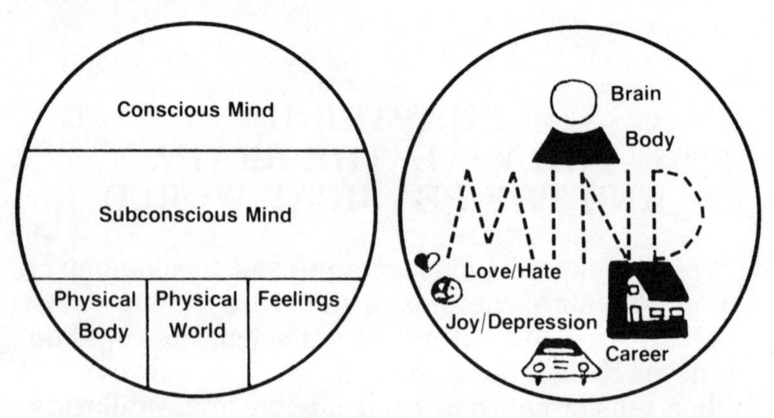

What we are saying here is that the brain, body, feelings, and the physical environment are all under the control of the mind. Your mind is you, your conscious awareness. It is what allows you to know about yourself and the world around you. It is the self of you. And your mind operates in a systematic, organized fashion.

First, you have a conscious mind. That is the part of your mind you are using as you read these words. Your conscious mind, which is about ten percent of your total mind, takes in information from your five senses, sight, sound, touch, taste, smell, and makes decisions about this information, storing that which it feels is significant in the memory cells of the brain for future use.

This is, of course, a simplistic explanation; however, it suits the purpose of this book, which is to move from a simple, theoretical framework to practical applications of principles that will enhance our lives. Thus, we will not be diverted from our task by exploring the difference between right and left brain activity, the multitude of mind-body theories, or the physiological intricacies of the brain. Suffice it to say that we believe your mind, your consciousness, that thing that makes you uniquely you, that which makes you aware of your environment controls your brain, body, and life experiences.

Your mind, the self of you, is not separate from your body or your affairs. It is in, through, and around you, and it works in the following manner.

CONSCIOUS MIND

We have already stated that our conscious mind takes input from your five senses, makes decisions about this information, and stores some of the information in the brain for further use. All of the information is stored in what, for our purposes, we call the subconscious mind. Some of the information is readily available, and some is more deeply stored in the subconscious. Very early in life we began making subjective decisions about the information and continue to do so to this day. The decisions we make about this information have labels attached to them. We begin by thinking in terms of good and bad, right and wrong, beautiful and ugly, nice and mean, positive and negative. This type of thinking becomes the basis of our belief systems about ourselves and our world. We become conscious of ourselves as thinking, feeling, unique beings interacting with our environment. However, our consciousness and belief systems are not developed by us alone. In fact, most of our belief systems are initially developed by messages received from others.

The first thing that happens is, we are born. Some people think that this is the first and foremost mistake, and if we had not been born, none of the other problems would have resulted. However, like it or not, we were born, and very rapidly we began receiving important and significant messages from others that impacted on the development of our conscious and subconscious belief systems.

For most of us, the first messages came from our parents. Some of those messages we rejected, but many of them we accepted. Those that we accepted became the building blocks of our belief systems. How we saw ourselves, how we saw others, and how we saw the world around us were all messages that affected our belief systems. Later we began to get another set of messages from our peers, and some of those messages conflicted with those given by our parents. We were then forced to make choices as to which messages would best apply to us. We received further messages in school, church, and other formal institutions with which we came into contact. Later in our lives we came into contact with jobs, politics, newspapers, televisions, law enforcement agencies, and so on. All of which gave us new and often contradictory messages.

If, particularly in our formative years, most of the messages we received and accepted were positive, fulfilling, confidence-building, the result is a fairly positive belief system. However, if many of the messages were negative, making us feel small while everything around us was large, the result is apt to be a negative belief system. Most of us have developed belief systems that contain some of each, positive and negative. This is the crux of the matter. We want to be able to eliminate the negative and accentuate the positive, and thus end up with more positive belief systems.

As a result of taking in so many different messages, we not only become a compilation of negative and positive beliefs, we also end up feeling somewhat fragmented. This is depicted in the example below:

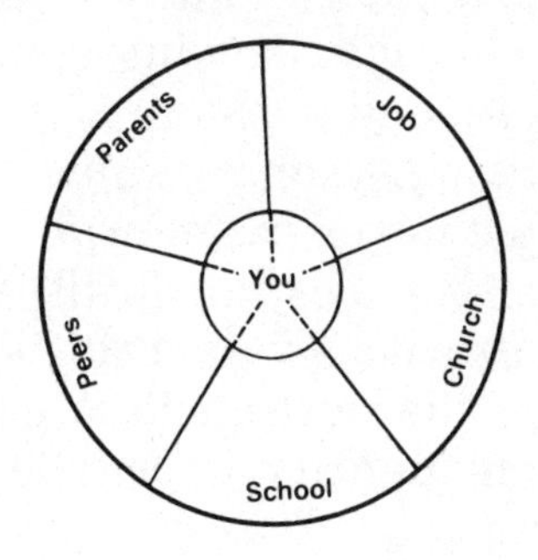

As we mature, we may feel somewhat torn apart or confused by all of the messages we have received. Some of us, in an attempt to deal with this, choose one set of messages and attempt to base our belief systems on that one piece of the pie, so to speak. In doing so, we are attempting to build a sense of identity in relationship to our now complicated belief systems.

We may become a gang member, gaining our identity from the group members and activities. Or we may choose the portions of our belief systems that have to do with work and become a worker person, whereby our identity comes from what we do for a living. Or we may decide to become a family person, in which case our identity comes from our home and family.

The problems that arise from picking one slice of the pie and basing our belief systems, and our identity, on that alone are twofold. First, the piece that we have chosen may come into conflict with other pieces. For instance, if we are a worker or career person, we might also have a family who puts demands on our time and energy, causing confusion and loss of identity. The second problem arises from the fact that, to be a whole person, we must incorporate all of the slices of pie into a meaningful whole. Just being a worker person does not fulfill all of our needs and also leaves us with a vulnerable identity. Should we lose our job, the bottom falls out of our belief systems, and our identity is crippled until we find another fulfilling job.

The crux of the matter is this: We want to build a set of belief systems that provide a whole, fulfilling sense of self, or identity. And we do this by eliminating the negative messages and accentuating the positive in every area of our lives, thus ending up with more positive belief systems. The reason we want to do this is because our belief systems control our conscious and subconscious mind, which in turn control our lives.

SUBCONSCIOUS MIND

It is important to know that the conscious mind includes only about ten percent of our mental resources. The subconscious, or below conscious, mind controls ninety percent of our mental resources. All of the information or messages we have accepted are stored in our subconscious. The subconscious mind also runs the autonomic nervous system of our body, our heart, digestion, breathing, and so on. The subconscious operates somewhat like a fantastic computer, storing all of the information one needs to operate successfully in the world. Aside from the autonomic nervous system, all information reaches the subconscious mind from the conscious mind. The conscious mind interprets information from the five senses and places significant information in the subconscious. Much of this information is readily available for future use, while some of it is stored deep in the subconscious and is more or less forgotten.

The conscious and subconscious mind work hand in glove to produce the results we experience in our physical body, our feelings, and our outer world. It is through the joint activity of these two parts of our mind that thoughts begin to become things. This is how, for instance, one learns to drive an automobile. First, we consciously decide we want to learn to drive. Then we find someone to teach us, and we consciously think about what we are doing. At first we have to think about how the gears work, the brake, the gas pedals. This information is rapidly passed to the subconscious mind for storage. In a short time, driving becomes automatic and we no longer have to consciously think about all of the separate operations. Now we simply decide we want to drive somewhere in our automobile. After making this decision, aside from a few corrective measures, we need to do very little conscious thinking about the operation of the automobile as we drive to our destination. We can be thinking about a thousand and one other things, visiting with friends, listening to the radio, and soon we have arrived where we originally decided to go. That is because our subconscious mind has taken over and produced for us the driving activity that we consciously stored there. The subconscious mind will continue to produce this activity automatically, unless it is consciously changed. In fact, the subconscious produces more satisfactorily without too much interference from the conscious mind. Once the decision is placed in the subconscious computer by the conscious mind, the subconscious computer will do its job automatically and successfully. If a police car pulls up behind us while we are driving, we often attempt to take over with our conscious mind because we think that by doing so we will have better control over the automobile. We try to let our foot off the clutch just right and accelerate at just the right speed and, of course, to appear absolutely innocent and casual to the policeman. The chances are we will stall the automobile halfway through the intersection. This is because we tried to take over consciously what the mind does best subconsciously. Too many times people try to do the job of the subconscious with the conscious mind. It is sort of like feeding a problem into a computer and then sitting down with paper and pencil to figure out the problem by hand.

The point we are making here is that once the decision has been made by the conscious mind, the subconscious mind will produce the right result. We make a decision to go to the store in our automobile. The subconscious takes over and with only a few conscious thoughts about driving we end up at the store. This is, in fact, how our entire life works. Whenever the subconscious information agrees with the conscious decisions or ideas, the result will automatically follow.

There are three important characteristics of the subconscious that we need to keep in mind. First, the basic nature of the subconscious is creative. Whatever is imprinted in the subconscious, the subconscious will strive to reproduce in our body, our feelings, our external affairs. Second, the subconscious is the power plant which brings our belief systems into reality. If the conscious input does not agree with the subconscious belief system, then the subconscious will produce according to the belief system, independent of the conscious input. Finally, the subconscious is subject to, and can be altered by, the conscious mind.

Therefore, suppose that we have consciously implanted automobile driving information in the subconscious. Based on this stored knowledge, the subconscious belief system is that we can drive a car, and that we have all of the knowledge and skill needed to do so. Being creative, the subconscious, at the direction of the conscious mind, will always automatically produce successful automobile driving activity. However, now suppose we go to England where they drive on the opposite side of the road and the gears and instruments are reversed. Our conscious mind must begin giving directions that are contrary to the subconscious right-hand driving belief system. For a period of time we will find that the subconscious automatically produces right-hand driving behavior, independent of our conscious instructions. Our right hand automatically reaches for the right-hand shift, our feet are all tangled up on the floor instruments, and we find ourselves going down the right side of the road, much to the consternation of the other drivers. However, with enough effort and practice, the conscious mind is able to change the belief system in the subconscious from right-hand to left hand driving. Then the subconscious will begin automatically to produce the proper driving behavior until we return home and are forced to change the subconscious belief system once again.

The same system applies to that friend of the working man or woman—the common cold or Monday morning flu. If we have taken enough "cold" messages into our subconscious belief system so that we now believe we get three or four colds every winter, that is exactly what will happen, regardless of the fact that we consciously would like not to have colds. Until we change the belief system, we will continue to produce colds in our lives. We may have also established additional belief systems that support our catching colds. We may have discovered early in life that we received more attention and love when we were sick, so periodically when we feel in need of attention and love, our subconscious belief system produces a cold as a means of getting the desired results. We may feel the only way we can take a day off is to be sick, so when we acutely feel the need for a day off, the subconscious belief system produces a cold. Since all of this is operating at a subconscious level away from our awareness, it becomes somewhat complicated. Fortunately, correcting subconscious belief systems is not complicated. This is because the subconscious can always be brought under control of the conscious mind. Belief systems can be, and are, changed by the conscious mind. We will discuss how to do this in detail later in the book.

OUR PHYSICAL WORLD

We have seen that we are continuously taking in information. Our conscious mind makes decisions about the information and gives it to our subconscious mind. If the information agrees with existing belief systems, the subconscious will immediately act upon it. If the information does not agree with existing belief systems, the subconscious will act on the belief systems rather than on the new conscious information. The action of the subconscious then appears as reality in our lives, in our bodies, in the way we feel emotionally, and in our external circumstances. Thus, what is going on inside of our heads will soon be going on in our world.

You and I are feeling the way we are today, making the amount of money, are healthy or sick, and have the kinds of relationships we have not because of outside circumstances, but because our thinking translated into belief systems has produced those things in our lives.

Far-fetched idea, you may be saying. Your first reaction may be, "I work hard, try to do and think the right things in the right way, and circumstances are always important factors in the results I get. A person with my education and background can only make so much money; the state of the economy is such that opportunities are limited; my boss does not like me; I have to support my family and their demands are something I can do nothing about. How did I, or how can I, create circumstances in my life over which it appears I have no control" Or you might be saying, "I have heard these ideas before. I tried out positive thinking and things got a little better, but I haven't gotten the really big or important things in my life, and it certainly appears that I am a victim of circumstances much of the time and this whole idea may be wishful thinking."

No one understands the skepticism expressed above better than I. I was the original negative thinker. I went around with a sure sense of "impending doom." I felt there was a ton of bricks around every corner waiting to fall on my head, and I was going to be sure to be there when they did. I had read positive thinking books and tried to do what they suggested. My field was sociology and psychology. I was supposed to know all about the human condition and how to improve it. Yet, I could not make any of my knowledge work in my own life. It appeared that the circumstances in my life had all of the power. People would not hire me because of my past troubles; I had difficulty relating to people; I was fearful and sick much of the time.

Then a friend of mine suggested I do two things. First, to begin reading positive thinking books that explained how it worked, and do this with an open mind. Second, write down as much as I was able to remember about the thinking process that preceded the significant events in my life, along with how I felt about myself at the time. I did as was suggested and discovered the thing I mentioned earlier. Every major event in my life was preceded by thinking on my part that could have led to no other conclusion. Also, I found I had some basic belief systems that could do nothing but wreak havoc in my life. I believed I was not as good as my peers. I believed that having a lot of money was wrong. I believed that pain and suffering were the lot of some people and that I was one of them. And on and on. And I saw the results of this type of thinking appearing in my life over and over with monotonous regularity.

Then I took a position that I would base my life for one year on the proposition that my thoughts created my internal and external world and see what happened. I decided that I had had all of the pain and suffering I was going to have in my life. I wrote down how I wanted my life to be in the areas of career, relationships, health, and finances. I determined to learn all I could about love, success, friendship, happiness, and freedom.

The result was that things immediately began to get better. At first I had doubts and would from time to time slip back into my old thinking patterns, but my belief systems were beginning to change and the results in my life were gratifying. It was through this process that I became convinced that the conscious mind, in conjunction with the subconscious mind, formulates belief systems that are indeed produced in our internal and external world. I began to see firsthand that if I believed a certain thing to be true, it would show up in my physical world. I believe this is the way it works for most of us. The only way we will know if the theories expressed in this book have any practical value is to test them. The second portion of this book will allow us to test the ideas and to prove to ourselves whether or not our belief systems are reproduced in our lives, externally as well as internally. And if we find this to be true, then we will know that we are not the victim of circumstances, but the creator of our own circumstances.

It is important to note here that the conscious mind is aware, or can be made aware quite easily of the belief systems an individual has, even though they are stored in the subconscious. We will find out how to do this also in a subsequent chapter.

Some of you are already using positive thinking techniques and are the better for it. However, you may have found, as I did, that some areas of your life just do not seem to be moving in the right direction. Or, it may be that the really important things appear to elude your grasp. So, while things are certainly getting better, they are not the best that they could be.

If this is the case, one of two things, or both, may be happening. The first is that you may not have identified and gotten rid of limited belief systems. The second may be that you do not realize the immensity of the power available to you, nor how to tap into that power. It is at this point we need to consider an idea which many of us try to avoid—a power greater than ourselves, and how it relates to us. Is there really a universal mind, and if so, what does that mean to us? For many of us, this sounds too spiritual or too mystical to be of any practical use. However, if we keep an open mind and consider the possibility of a larger power contained within us, permeating the atmosphere around us, and working according to natural law, we might very well be able to make a breakthrough in making our lives the very best we can imagine. Also, if there is such a power and if we can come to understand it, we will have an explanation as to how thoughts become things.

CHAPTER III
UNIVERSAL MIND AND POWER

When we begin talking about spiritual issues, or spiritual power, everyone starts to get nervous, or skeptical, or just plain not interested. I understand these kinds of feelings. I have had them all. However, we agreed to keep an open mind throughout this book. Someone once said, "A closed mind is the surest way to everlasting ignorance", and I have found that to be painfully true from time to time in my life.

Let us make one thing clear from the beginning. It was stated earlier and it is necessary to say it again. When we talk about spirituality in this book, we are not talking about religion. I have no authority to discuss religious issues, nor do I wish to do so. We are talking here about a power that might exist in this universe, which is positive and which we might be able to use; and we are discussing a concept of how that power might work so that we can apply it in our own lives according to the principles we have already learned, to move from where we are now to where we want to be.

This power has been called universal mind, universal intelligence, God, the great spirit, energy, power, and a great many other things. Whatever fits you best is the terminology you should use. We are going to use several terms interchangeably in this book that all mean the same thing—a power in this universe that is available for you to use to get what you want in your life.

Let us suppose then, for the sake of argument, that in the beginning there was some sort of first cause. An intelligent force or spirit, if you please, which had the power to create. Since there was no matter—no physical things—in existence, this force would have to create things out of the invisible stuff of which itself was made. Let us further suppose then that it did just that. It began to think about worlds and planets and stars, and out of its own thought these things were somehow created.

Many people believe that behind those tiny particles called atoms there is an even more ethereal substance, and that this substance is first cause, and is how first cause creates. Whether or not we believe this idea, we know today that what we call energy and matter are interchangeable.

We can see this idea for ourselves by taking invisible vapor, condensing it into water, and then freezing the water into solid matter. The thing that was unseen is transformed by a form of energy into a solid object with all of the original properties still contained within it.

The importance of this idea for our purpose is twofold. First, whatever first cause created, the essential parts of first cause are contained within the created thing, because it makes everything out of itself. Therefore, first cause or universal intelligence and power, is contained in and through everything that exists, including you and me. Second, things are created through a law of cause and effect. First cause, or universal intelligence, thinks about what it wants to create. The thinking is cause. Then those thoughts, moving through energy, become things. The things are effect. The significance of this conceptual base will become clear as we go on.

Now consider for a moment, again for the sake of argument, that you and I are creating in our own small universe in the same way that first cause or universal mind is creating in the larger universe. And that human beings are able to create things out of their thoughts because of their unique relationships to universal mind. Finally, that human beings, you and I, because of our unique relationships to universal mind, have much more power to create than we previously suspected. Let's see how and in what way this might work.

If we take our diagram of the individual mind and expand it, it might look something like this:

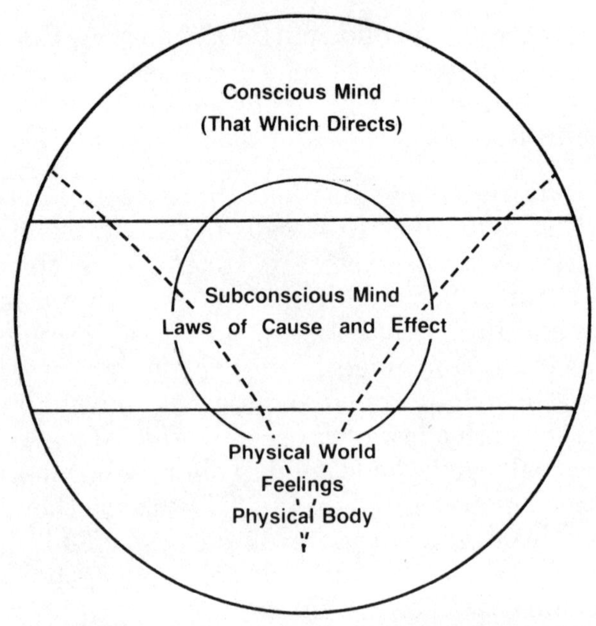

In this diagram, the larger circle indicates the Universal Mind; the smaller circle denotes You.

The diagram represents the fact that our individual being is part of a larger whole. The larger whole being universal mind. The significance here is, not only does our own mind create in the same way as the larger universal mind, but it does so within the context of a universal creative medium which is around and through us. That which is contained in the larger creative experience in the universe is also contained within us. Many people feel this is what is meant by being made in the image of God. It is this being part and parcel of the larger universal mind, that allows our minds to create our own smaller universe.

What happens is this. Our conscious mind begins a train of thought. This thought goes into our subconscious mind. If the subconscious belief systems are in tune with the thought and do not contradict it, the thought moves into the larger subconscious mind, which is the creative medium through which a corresponding result is produced in our physical world. This is because our mind is part of the larger universal mind; so, in effect, we are actually using a part of the larger mind when we are using our own mind. There is, in actuality, no separation between our mind and the universal mind, but all of the elements of the universal creative mind are contained within our own mind. In addition, we are able to use the power of the larger mind in our creative efforts because we are part of it and able to use much greater power than is contained within our own mind.

We might compare the human mind's relationship to the universal mind as a drop of water to the ocean. The drop of water contains all the elements of the ocean within itself, and when emersed in the ocean becomes one with the ocean, and vice versa. Another comparison can be seen in the tiny seed that we place in the ground. The seed immediately begins to draw upon the elements and nutrients surrounding it. Soon it bursts its tiny shell, and although it is developing an identity of its own, this identity contains the elements that surrounded the seed as it became a plant. As it bursts through the soil, it incorporates more universal elements from the sun, rain, and air until it blooms as an individual identity. But the individual plant still contains within itself the elements of its surrounding universe.

When we transfer this idea to the mental plain, we can see, assuming our basic premise is correct, that the mind we use is a part of universal mind, and is in fact doing the same thing that universal mind is doing. It is thinking thoughts, and through the law of cause and effect, those thoughts become things. How do the thoughts become things? They go into the universal subconscious mind and convert energy into matter.

The human mind, being part and parcel of the universal mind, does the same thing as the universal mind. We think thoughts and they go through our subconscious into the universal subconscious and convert energy into matter. Our own mind, working within universal mind, becomes cause in our own world; and the circumstances we see in our world are the effects of what we have caused by our thoughts. If we follow this premise to its logical conclusion, our thoughts are always causing results in our world. Again, this idea may seem rather far-fetched at first glance. Again, you might want to consider the idea of thoughts becoming things in light of your own experience. Look at some of your past experiences, especially the significant things that have happened in your life. See if you can remember the thinking and the belief systems that preceded certain events or experiences. You should be able to see definite patterns of thought that could have led to nothing other than what happened. If it does not become clear to you at this time, do not worry. Later in the book you will have an opportunity to test out this theory in your present situation.

Human beings also create by using another law based on the law of cause and effect. It is called the law of attraction. Since our world is already made up of people, places, and things, we do not often have to create new things out of our thoughts. What often happens is that our thoughts, based on subconscious belief systems, go into the universal subconscious and attract to us people, places, or things according to our thinking. For many people this is a less far-fetched law because it can be more easily seen. If tomorrow you go around all day acting grumpy and treating everyone with hostility, you will not be surprised to observe that you receive a great deal of hostility in return. On the other hand, if you are cheerful and friendly towards everyone you meet, a greater proportion of cheerfulness and friendliness will be returned to you. This is a simplistic example of the law of attraction. It is operating through the law of cause and effect. You begin with your thoughts, which in turn lead you into certain types of behavior and activity which result in your world being a certain way.

Now, since we are part of universal mind, our thoughts are both creating and attracting on a greater scale than simply people, places, and things with whom we come into physical contact. Operating through the universal subconscious mind, our thoughts are attracting results in our lives from far and wide.

For example, if we are seeking a certain type of employment and we subconsciously believe we can have that type of employment, the law of cause and effect will be working in one of two ways. The job may already exist. If so, our original thought will direct us to do the things that might obtain for us such a position. Our thoughts and belief systems will be connecting with and attracting us to the person who has the job and we will soon be brought together through the law of attraction. If, however, the job as we envision it does not exist, and if we insist that our thoughts and belief systems remain on the job we want, the job can and will be literally created for us. I have seen this proven again and again in my own life and in the lives of countless others.

If the laws of cause and effect work in the ways described above, the implication is of a magnitude which, at first, appears incredible. It means that through laws as specific and immutable as those of gravity and electricity, we are at this moment, through our thinking, creating the circumstances that will show up in our lives tomorrow; and whatever is going on in our lives today was created by our thoughts yesterday, last week, or last year. In fact, if this is so, it not only applies to the amount of money we are making, the kind of career we have, our relationships with others, but also how we feel mentally and physically. It means there is no depression, for instance, floating around in the air that we catch; rather, the thoughts and belief systems we place in our subconscious mind result in a feeling of depression. Furthermore, our depressive thoughts then go out into the universal subconscious and attract depressing circumstances to reinforce our feelings of depression. The same thing applies to physical well-being or illness.

If we accept that this is the way things work, it places a great deal of responsibility on us as the arbiters of our own world. It means that we are producing our situations directly from our thoughts and belief systems; therefore, if we want our lives to be a certain way, we must keep our thoughts in line with what we want to feel and want to have happen.

As we mentioned earlier, most of us either do not know, or do not do anything about the fact that our thoughts and feelings are under our own control. We are often thinking one thing, believing another, and doing a third. We arise in the morning and say, "I really want to have a good day on the job today and get the promotion I deserve." But by the time we have struggled through the morning rush hour in traffic and listened to the terrible state of the economy on the radio, we allow our thoughts to become somewhat irritable. Then we see the boss and our co-workers and remember how much we dislike the boss, how unfair he is, and the same goes for several of our co-workers. By now all thoughts of a good day have been negated, and we start thinking in terms of surviving another day among the incompetence and aggravation which we are forced to tolerate to earn our living. Little wonder, if our thoughts are creating, that we end up with results other than our original purpose. We feel we are victims of circumstance, and that our environment needs to be radically changed. It is, however, our thoughts that need to be changed.

Suppose we then accept the premise that we must change our thinking patterns. What then? How, under such negative circumstances, can we change our thinking? First, we have to remember that we have, in effect, created the circumstances in which we find ourselves. We may balk at that idea. We did not make the boss such an unfair, irritable person. No, but our previous thinking and belief system landed us the present job with all of its positive and negative aspects attached. O.K., we say, before we rush out and quit our job, we will try taking control of our thinking process for awhile and see what happens. And an incredible thing happens. We find out just how difficult the task of controlling our thinking is. This is because we have, for so long, given our mind free reign to think whatever it pleases. So we make a determined effort to think positively and keep our goals firmly in mind all day, but with amazing rapidity and regularity the old thought patterns intrude.

If you want to test this, try the following exercise. Find a quiet place, relax and clear your mind of all distracting thoughts. Then breathe in and count one. Continue this through four, then start over. See how long you can think of your breathing and the numbers until another thought intrudes. The multitude of other thoughts that interfere with your intended concentration will give you an idea of how much of your thinking seems to operate independently of your control. However, the task of controlling your thinking is not insurmountable—far from it. We will be talking later in the book on precisely how to control our thinking to our advantage. Remember, we are supposed to be in control of our thoughts and feelings. It is just that we have not exercised that control as effectively as we might have; thus, our thoughts have been creating, without purposeful direction, much of the time. Therefore, most of what is going on in our lives appears to be discordant or beyond our control. We do not need to control the circumstances in our lives; we only need to control our thoughts, which are cause, to either control or change the circumstances.

Even those of us who have gained some control over our thinking processes often fail to realize the potential of being part and parcel of the universal mind, and we use the power contained in the law of cause and effect in a very limited way. That brings us to the crux of this chapter—universal power.

UNIVERSAL MIND

If you refer to the chart on page 28, you will see a diagram of what has been repeated several times thus far— that you and I are emersed so to speak, in a universal intelligence or mind. We are not separate from the universal mind in any way. In fact, the mind you are using right now is a part of the universal mind. This means, in effect, that everything is "one thing." The one thing being universal mind, which created everything and remains within everything. The idea of oneness is sometimes difficult to grasp. What does it mean when we say you and I and everyone and everything are one? You are an individual, and I am an individual, and we certainly appear to be using our own separate minds. So, how can we be one? It does not seem to make sense.

Some people believe that the only way universal intelligence can express itself is to create itself in human form and we are thus expressions of this universal mind; that humans have the same power of choice that universal mind has, and can exercise that power of choice to create or express in any manner they choose. Thus, individuality is created and protected. At the same time, the universal mind resides in and around each individual, making them one with the universal intelligence, but never losing their power of choice, nor their individuality.

For those of us who have grown up in some formal religious or spiritual system, these ideas may appear foreign or contrary to what we have been taught. For some of us the idea that God, or spirit, or universal mind is contained right within us, as well as around us, may be disconcerting and confusing. We may need to think about, argue with, and investigate, until it makes sense to us individually. We may want to do some additional reading to clarify this idea and reconcile it with our existing beliefs. One of the best books on the oneness of ourselves and universal mind is The Edinburgh Lectures, by Thomas Troward, published by Dodd, Mead, and Company, New York, N.Y. Although the book was written in 1909, it is still in print and remains one of the best explanations of the ideas heretofore expressed.

Of course, the final conclusion to be drawn from the above premise is that the power of God or spirit or universal intelligence is contained within each individual, and the individual can use this power; and in fact we are using this power all of the time because it is the only power there is. Without using the power of universal mind, our hearts would not beat, our food would not turn into hair, fingernails, bones, muscles, and tissue. Of course, this is not a new idea by any means. Philosophers and teachers throughout the ages have taught that there is more to man and woman than meets the eye. From Aristotle to Einstein, from Jesus to Emerson, the idea of a life force larger than man, but contained within man, has been expressed. Great achievers from Alexander the Great, through Abraham Lincoln, to Henry Ford felt that they were using a power greater than themselves and contained within themselves.

At this point we need to take a few moments to consider the basic elements of the universal power of which we have said we are a part. Universal mind is felt to be creative, as we have already seen. Its basic nature is one of creativity, and the basic structure of the universe supports life and growth. It is also intelligent, and its intelligence permeates all things. This intelligence is what causes atoms and molecules to form in a certain way to produce everything from human bodies to heavenly bodies. That which causes roots of plants to seek nutrients, and the process that transforms these nutrients into the completed result, is intelligence. Since the plants themselves do not have intelligence as we think of it, then they must contain universal intelligence.

Universal mind, or intelligence, is orderly and logical. This underlying orderliness is what keeps the planets and stars in orbit. It is what makes the seasons change. It is what causes the carrot seed to become a carrot and not a pumpkin or an ear of corn.

Universal mind is power—all of the power that can be imagined. It is the power contained in the wind, the rain, and the snow. It is the mighty power of the ocean, the amazing power of electricity, and the stabilizing power of gravity.

Universal intelligence is beauty and harmony. Because the universe is well ordered, it results in the beautiful. Things that are in tune with this universal harmony are said to contain beauty, whether it be the majestic mountains or the fragile rose.

Universal intelligence is also unlimited abundance. When it creates, it creates in staggering amounts and is capable of creating over and over in inexhaustible supply. There is always more than enough. In this case we may ask, "What about the world's diminishing fuel supplies?" I have no doubt, even with man's wasteful use of these natural resources, universal intelligence through mankind's intelligence will provide combinations of elements to solve this problem. Of course, in the scheme of things, orderly non-wasteful use of resources is the way to stay in tune with universal supply and abundance.

Universal mind is also that magic word we call love. The universe, the world, life itself appear to be based on a loving concept. Everything in our world supports life, growth, beauty, and well-being. The world is ordered in a fashion that love can be seen as the underlying principle. Everything has been provided to allow mankind to operate successfully within this magnificent environment. It is only man's belief in lack and limitation that causes the opposite of love to be seen in the world.

Universal mind is much more than has been described above, since it is in and around everything, and in fact, it is all there is. However, the limited descriptions we have considered should give us some idea of the nature of universal intelligence. Its power and magnificence are all around us and within us. As I ate my breakfast this morning, I did so with the confidence that the food would be distributed throughout my body, that the vitamins and minerals would go to the right places, and that fuel would be produced for me to do whatever was needed during my day. I do not know how that all takes place, but universal intelligence does. And it does it automatically, all of the time. As I look around my study, I see the beauty of woodgrain all around me, created by universal mind and made even more magnificent by human hands. As I observe the incredible craftsmanship of that unknown man or woman who used their talents to produce a beautiful object that gives me pleasure every day of my life, I sense a oneness with them. This oneness comes from each of us being one with the universal intelligence, using the one mind to express our individual talents and abilities.

Of course, each of us must decide what universal mind is for ourselves. We must take these general ideas and apply them to ourselves personally. For our purposes, we must also clarify what universal mind does—how it works.

Universal mind, God, spirit, is creative. It creates out of its own thinking and self by the use of laws, which are as specific and immutable as the laws governing gravity or electricity. The overall law is the law of cause and effect. Universal mind thinks something. That thought goes into the universal subjective and creates substance, which is the effect. The substance is created through the law of growth. This simply means that there is a time factor between the original thought and the formation of the substance to be produced. The growth period works in conjunction with natural laws. An example might be the acorn, which has all of the basic elements of an oak tree within itself, put there by universal mind, but must go through a growth period to realize its full potential. There are things we can do to expedite and shorten the growth period, but there is always a time factor involved. The creative process also utilizes a law of attraction. At first there was no form or matter; therefore, there was nothing to attract. But as universal intelligence used its self-thinking to produce form, the law of growth took over and expanded the universal substance so that at our stage of evolution all of the elements to create whatever is needed now exist, with universal intelligence contained within them. This allowed the law of attraction to evolve. Therefore, the acorn in becoming an oak tree is attracted to and attracts to itself the elements of the soil, air, and water to develop and grow into the thing it is meant to be.

This cursory glance at what universal mind is and how it works should be helpful in understanding a power greater than ourselves. You may be saying at this point that is all very interesting, but how does all of this relate to me and my life? We have talked a bit about how your mind works and how the universal mind works. Let's see if we can now tie the whole thing together so that these concepts will relate to you personally and so that you will be able to use them to your advantage.

I hope I will not exasperate you too badly by asking you to refer back to the diagram on page 28, and involving you in what may appear to be unnecessary repetition. I feel, however, that it is important for us to be clear on our theoretical base before we begin the practical application.

In our diagram and our discussion heretofore we have seen that universal mind and our own minds work in precisely the same way. As far as we know, humans are the only species who have this unique facility. Thus, we are not separate from universal mind, but are a part of it. If this is true, we have an incredible amount of power at our beckoned call. This should mean we can create anything we want to in our lives just by thinking the right thoughts. Our conscious mind selects and directs the thoughts into the subconscious mind, which through the law of cause and effect automatically produces the results. If this is the case, then why are we not creating exactly what we want in our lives all of the time? There are several reasons for this, all of which can be corrected. We will not only discuss why we are not creating properly, but also precisely what to do to correct that situation. All of the problems in creating properly stem from our lack of knowledge of universal mind and our relationship to it.

The first problem has already been discussed. Many of us had no knowledge that our thoughts were creating, therefore, we did not attempt to direct our thoughts in any particular way most of the time.

Another problem has a direct relationship with our lack of knowledge concerning universal mind and power. Most of us, even those who are optimistic and think positively, use the power we have available in a limited way. We stay within our own small circle, particularly on the conscious level, so that we are giving rather limited directions to the subconscious creative medium and thus, our results are limited. The important thing to remember here is that since we are part and parcel of the universal mind, we can actually connect, and in fact are always connected with the universal mind on a conscious level, thereby removing the limitations from the thoughts we give to the subconscious medium. More than that, we can get guidance and direction from the conscious part of universal mind. We can tap into vast amounts of knowledge contained therein, which allows us to expand our conscious belief systems concerning the amount of anything we wish created in our lives, whether it be happiness, abundance, or right relationships.

It is as if we are in a darkened house with a small flashlight. We can certainly move about the house and get done the things we need to do by the beam of our flashlight, but it is quite difficult. How much better to turn on the light switches and illuminate the entire house. Now we can move about quite freely and easily and we can do much more. This is an analogy of what we can do in our own lives. We can break out of our own small conscious speculations and connect with the larger universal mind at any time we wish. We do not have to go anywhere or look long and far, because our mind is already a part of universal mind and that means that universal mind is already within us. We have always been using universal mind, but in a very limited way. Now we want to remove the limitations we ourselves have placed, or have allowed others to place, on universal mind within us. There is only one power in, through, and around everything, including us. We are always using it in a limited or unlimited way, a positive or negative way; it is all the same power and we can use as much of it as we will. It is available to us as unlimited knowledge, health, energy, wealth, and love. It is all of these things and so are we, because we are one with the power.

This idea is a change from a far-off diety, separate from ourselves, who sits in judgement on us and our activities. It is also different from the idea of a diety or God with whom we must plead, so that he will give us what we want. We have already been given the power to have anything we want through the system of spiritual law we have heretofore been talking about. Some of us may have to reconsider the old ideas of sin, suffering, reward, punishment, based on whether we are being good or bad. It would appear, according to the philosophy we have been discussing, that you and I are responsible for the evil we find in our lives as a result of how we have been using the law. We may wish to argue with this idea at first, stating that we certainly did not want unpleasant things to happen in our lives, and are not going to take responsibility for them. However, if we consider the belief systems we had at the time, we will often be able to see that they were not in tune with what we said we wanted to happen, and in fact were more in tune with what did happen.

The idea then is for us to become connected with the universal mind and to use its power more specifically and in less limited manner than we have been doing up to this point. There are two things going on within this power simultaneously. First, there is universal intelligence, of which we are a part. The thing for us to do is to become connected with this universal intelligence in a conscious manner. Because in so doing, we remove the limited thinking we have imposed upon ourselves and contact unlimited intelligence and power. We in effect turn the lights on. There is nothing magical or mystical in doing this. Since we are already a part of the universal intelligence, we do not have to go anywhere or do anything special to contact it. We simply need to consciously contemplate the fact that universal mind and our own minds are one in the same. This opens our receptivity so that we can get inspiration, intuitive thoughts, guidance and direction from universal mind. All of the knowledge of the universe is contained in universal mind; being part of it, this knowledge is also available to us. We need only open our minds to it. In the next chapter, we will not only come to understand the above proposition, but will actually experience it.

The main consideration is, if we can connect with the larger intelligence from the very beginning, we will be able to remove limitation from our thinking and be able to use much more of the universal intelligence and power. Remember, this power is not "out there" somewhere, but right within us, right now. The mind I am using to write these words, and the mind you are using to read them is in fact the universal mind within us. We simply want to use more of that larger mind.

The second thing going on with universal mind is that it is, as we have already said, continually creating through the laws of cause and effect. Thoughts go into the universal creative medium, which we have been calling the universal subconscious, and result in things being created or produced in the physical world. That includes us. We are created out of the material of universal mind, and are in the unique position of being able to create in the same way, using the same creative material and creative process.

Since we are part and parcel of universal intelligence, we are not creating independently. This is an important point to consider, for we do not want to get the idea that we are making or forcing our own thoughts to create the desired results. We are using universal power from beginning to end, the same way we use the laws of gravity or electricity. We do not need to make anything happen. We simply need to connect with the universal intelligence, decide what it is we desire, and let the universal creative medium produce the results. We will see just how this works and how we can prove this theory to ourselves in the following chapters.

CHAPTER IV
FORMULA FOR POSITIVE CHANGE

If we wish to tap into a universal power and use that power to not only improve our lives, but to make our lives everything we would desire them to be, what do we need to do? We need, first and foremost, to change or to expand our belief systems. We have stated that it is not what we wish, want, or hope for, that is created in our lives, but rather, that which we believe to be true about ourselves and our world. We use universal creative intelligence only in accordance with our own basic belief systems, because that is the way the law of cause and effect works. Thoughts, backed by belief systems, are the cause of the circumstances in our lives. We need to have, or develop, attitudes that support a happy, healthy, overall belief system. To do this we need to identify and evaluate the belief systems we have at the present time. Before we can effectively change anything we need to know what it is that needs to be changed, and if in fact it needs changing. We may find it simply needs revision or expansion.

Step One then is: Identifying and Evaluating Belief Systems.

We have already seen how we develop our belief systems by taking information from our environment, making decisions about that information, and then applying it to ourselves and our world. Our belief systems combine to give us a basic attitude towards ourselves and our relationship to the world. For instance, when we are children we see that we are small while everything and everyone around us is big. As we grow into adulthood, this idea should change so that we see ourselves as being as big as everyone else and able to cope with most things around us. However, many of us do not adequately make this transition, so we carry the idea that we are small and everyone else is big into our adult lives, or we may feel small in relation to certain individuals or things. If this is the case, we develop belief systems that will affect our overall attitude toward ourselves and will limit the way in which we use the creative power that is available to us. We will tend to be fearful and anxious when dealing with certain individuals or things. We may deny this fact to ourselves to remain comfortable, nevertheless, we will be limited in expressing our potential until that belief system is changed. This is so because the ideas we formulate, based on our belief systems, are continually showing up in our world as a result of the laws of cause and effect. Any belief system, whether we feel it is positive or negative, results in certain circumstances being created in our lives. Our beliefs about money, work, relationships, love, health, and so on, are all being experienced in what we call reality.

Many of us have attempted to change this situation through our spiritual or religious ideas. We have prayed to God or a higher power to intercede and change things for us. When they were not changed, we felt our prayers were not answered. Some of us even lost our faith. Others of us have tried to do things we felt would please our particular diety, feeling that was the way to get the results we desired. In actuality, our prayers were not answered because we were asking for a spiritual law, which is as specific as the natural law of gravity, to be changed or usurped. That kind of prayer is much the same as my praying for the desk at which I am sitting to rise to the ceiling. I would be asking for a violation of the law of gravity. The chances of such a prayer getting results are nil. If I really wanted the desk to rise to the ceiling and stay there, it could be done. I would need to use the law of gravity along with other natural laws, in the proper way, to get the job done. With ropes and pulleys I could fairly easily suspend the desk from the ceiling. By working with natural laws, mankind makes iron ships float, flies in the air, and explores space. The example I used seems silly, of course. The point being made here is that we must work within the scope of spiritual and natural law if we are to consistently obtain the results we desire. We have already been given all of the power we need to have whatever we want. We simply need to use the laws of cause and effect in the proper way. Since whatever is in our life is a result of our belief systems, if we do not have precisely what we want, we need to change our belief systems so they are more in line with what we do want. The right belief systems will cause the right conditions to appear. This is an immutable law.

If faulty belief systems cause faulty use of the power within us and create faulty conditions in our lives, how can we know what those belief systems are and how can we correct them? First, we need to look at the conditions in our lives and decide which are the way we want them to be, and which are not. Those conditions that are highly satisfactory are a result of good, solid, positive belief systems. Those conditions that are not so satisfactory are a result of poor, faulty, or negative belief systems.

If you are feeling that all but one or two areas of your life are highly satisfactory, or if you feel none of the areas of your life are very satisfactory, the same things applies. Your life situation is a result, directly or indirectly, of your belief systems. I want to stress the words highly satisfactory. Your life is not supposed to be just O.K., it is supposed to be great in every area. This is no "Pollyanna" idea. We are being practical and pragmatic. The greater your belief system, the greater your life.

As we explore the conditions of our lives, we may run into the problem, previously discussed, of not wanting to take responsibility for the unsatisfactory areas of our lives. We do not want to feel we have belief systems that would cause us unpleasant results. However, if we take an honest look at the situation, we may be able to see how we have had much more to do with the way things are than we think. If we have belief systems that tell us we are small and everything else is big, that we have no special talents, that others have power over us, that employers never appreciate employees, that all wealthy people are selfish and greedy, that people are usually competitive and unfeeling, that men are always chauvinistic in the workplace, that women are not good workers, then we should not be surprised that some areas of our lives are not working as well as we would like. Whether we want to believe it or not, these kinds of belief systems, through the law of cause and effect, produce negative results in our lives. We do not want to make the mistake of putting the cart before the horse. We did not accidentally get into unpleasant situations and then respond with negative belief systems. The negative belief systems came first, the negative conditions are the result.

Looking honestly at our belief systems is not always an easy task. Sometimes we have to be almost brutally honest with ourselves, putting aside the wrongs of others, and accepting the fact that our own belief systems are the basis for the people, places and things we have attracted into our lives. However, the rewards of doing so are incredible. When we identify our faulty belief systems we can rapidly change them. As a result our lives will rapidly change, not only for the better, but for the best. People, places and things will lose their power over us, and we will effectively be using our inner power, seeing it demonstrated in outer greatness.

In the following chapters we are going to discuss specific methods for identifying and evaluating our belief systems. We will see precisely how to change and expand our belief systems so that we are producing exactly what we want in our lives. It has been my experience that when the belief systems are changed, the battle has already been won. Ninety percent of our problems lie in this area. Therefore, identifying and getting rid of faulty belief systems is paramount if we are to make positive changes.

The Second Step in positive change consists of Setting Goals.

Once we have established that we can have what we want, we then have to know what it is we want. At first glance this appears to be a simple step, but that is not always the case. The old adage, be careful what you ask for because you might get it, has now changed to—you will get it. In fact, through the law of cause and effect, you have always been getting it, for better or for worse. Now we not only want to make it for better, but—for best. So we need to take some time in deciding what it is that we really want to see expressed in our lives. We also need to know how to get rid of limiting ideas concerning what we can have, because in fact we can have it all.

Some of us may find we have difficulty deciding what we really want. We may have feelings that it is selfish to want too much. We may have wants that appear to conflict with others, or contain elements of risk within them. We need, then, to reconsider some of our basic premises. Universal mind has provided, and is continually providing, more than enough to go around. How much one has is not a matter of selfish or unselfish, but a matter of correct or incorrect use of the laws of cause and effect, attraction and growth. Also, we need not think of the things we want today as being immutable or forever. There is no law against changing one's mind.

At any rate, sooner or later we will need to establish goals — what do we want? In this way we direct the law of cause and effect, and use the universal power in a given direction, to produce specific results in our lives. Otherwise, we are using the law in a non-directive manner and the results in our lives are non-specific and general. If we want our lives to be all that they can be, we need to decide what would make them so, and then make a decision that that is what we want.

We will also discuss this step in detail later in the book so we will know how to make the best decisions and goals for each of us individually.

The Third Step in positive change is Releasing the Goal.

The idea here is to turn the desired goal over to the universal subconscious law, as shown in the diagram on page 28. The law of cause and effect then goes into operation, and through the laws of growth and attraction, the goal will be realized. This does not mean we will forget all about our goal. We must keep our goal firmly in mind, but we must also understand that the law of cause and effect is producing the results. As soon as we decide on our goal the things needed to produce our goal are, if they exist, being attracted to us and we are being attracted to them. If things or conditions are needed to produce our goal and they do not yet exist, they are then through the law of growth, being created so that our goal can be realized. Since we will be operating out of new or expanded belief systems, this idea will no longer appear to be as far-fetched as it was in the beginning. When we experiment and find the results to be satisfactory, our belief in, and our ability to use these principles will be reinforced.

Step Four in the process is: Take Some Action Towards Realizing the Goal.

If we have, in step three, turned the goal over to the law of cause and effect, and it is producing the goal, why do we need to do anything more? Why can we not sit in our living rooms, decide what we want, and wait for the results? In fact, if our consciousness, our belief systems, were unlimited and in perfect harmony with universal law, we could probably do just that—produce any result in our lives without effort on our part. However, few of us, in fact none of us, has a consciousness so perfected as to operate in such a manner. At the same time, the action we will be taking may be quite different than our actions of the past.

Much of the action we will now be taking toward our goal will be done at home. We will be doing things like meditating on our goal, visualizing it, and acting as if we already have it. This will have the effect of reinforcing our commitment to attaining our goal. One of the things we need to do is to reinforce our desire for a given goal. We do this by increasing its importance to us. The more significance we attach to a goal, the more impetus it will have in the universal law, and the sooner it will be realized. This is similar to adding water and nourishment to a seed we have planted.

In addition to the type of action described above, we will be doing something else. We will be paying attention to what is happening around us. Once we have placed our goal in universal subconscious law, we simply need to watch for indications of the direction we should take in realizing our goal. We will then be guided, so to speak, in the type of action we are to take. Someone will mention something concerning a way to obtain our goal, we will read something that concerns our goal, or certain circumstances will appear to be leading us in a particular direction. These are the laws of growth and attraction at work.

Finally, we will take the action that seems normal and reasonable at the time. If our goal is a certain type of job, we might look in the want ads, send our resumes, and tell people we are in the market for that type of work. However, we do not want to get caught up in this type of action. We do not want to rush around job-hunting and sending resumes to the extent we do not see the subtle working of the universal laws, which are, in fact, attracting the job to us and us to it. We do a minimum of job-hunting and a maximum of working on our belief systems and paying attention to what, in our world of affairs, appears to be leading us to our goal.

The Fifth Step is: Enjoy the Process.

Many of us, when we set a goal become so goal-oriented that we feel we will not be happy until we obtain that particular goal. Therefore, our daily activities are seen only as means to an end, and become drab and uninteresting. We want to avoid this at all costs. If we do not enjoy the process in reaching our goal, there is a very good chance we will not enjoy the realization of our goal either.

Most of us take ourselves and the situations in which we find ourselves far too seriously. This results in our not having nearly enough fun in our lives. It also results in giving people, places and things power over how much enjoyment we allow ourselves.

You may feel at this time that you have problems

in your life which are much too serious to be taken lightly. We are not denying the reality of these kinds of problems or conditions in your life. They are real and the situation needs to be changed. This is what this book is all about. However, if we can accept the idea that our belief systems led us to where we are today, including all of our problems, and that we can change those belief systems, and when we do, our lives will change accordingly and the problems will be resolved, then the problems begin to take on a more reasonable and less overwhelming complexion.

The important thing to begin knowing is that the conditions which are so troublesome at present are not permanent and were attracted into our lives by certain belief systems, and we are now changing our belief systems; thus, the conditions will change. This knowledge allows us to take a much more hopeful and cheerful attitude in the midst of our present situation, because we have sure knowledge that our conditions will soon change for the better.

The five points or steps discussed in this chapter will connect us with the universal power that is contained within us, and allow us to use that power to make positive changes in our lives. This inner power will be released and then we can use it to have and be anything we wish. In the following chapters we will dissect these five steps and see how to use them specifically to create positive change immediately and continuously.

PART TWO
THE PRACTICE

CHAPTER V
CHANGING AND EXPANDING BELIEF SYSTEMS

According to what we have said so far, that which you believe to be true about yourself and your life is being produced in your world. The way you feel right now physically and emotionally, your financial condition, your relationships with others, are all results of your basic belief systems. If certain areas of your life are going great, it is because you have great belief systems in those areas. If some parts of your life are not so good, it is because your belief systems are not so good.

Therefore, we need a system whereby we can identify faulty belief systems and get rid of them. If we can do this, we will be able to replace the limiting belief systems with ones that are in line with our goals. Many of us have tried to put positive thinking on top of old negative belief systems, and have found that it does not work well, if at all. The old belief systems that have been reinforced over a period of time have tremendous power and continue to produce results based on their content, regardless of the new thinking we attempt to introduce. And the only way to change anything is to know what it is we wish to change. So, how do we go about doing that?

There are two ways to identify and change belief systems. The first is to evaluate which ones are faulty; then going through a process to change those beliefs identified as faulty into something more workable. The second is to look at what we are doing or feeling to create and reinforce faulty belief systems. Both methods are needed to effect permanent change.

We need to deal with what we are doing to reinforce faulty belief systems first, because unless we are able to take corrective measures in this area, we will have difficulty in dealing with the actual belief systems in a constructive way.

THE BASIS FOR HEALTHY BELIEF SYSTEMS

First of all, we all wish to be happy, healthy people; because if we are, our belief systems will tend to be happy and healthy, and the results produced in our lives will be positive. Therefore, we need to identify what constitutes a happy, healthy person.

There are certain conditions necessary for anyone who wants to be happy, healthy, and have his or her life work successfully.

The first condition required of a healthy individual is self-worth. We must have a sense that we are O.K.

within ourselves, as well as within our world, regardless of what others are thinking or doing. We must have a feeling that we are in tune with ourselves. If we have this, we will have what is commonly called self-confidence. We will be able to relate to our environment in a sure and positive way. We will be able to make decisions based on the reality of our situation, and have the power to act intelligently on those decisions. We will be able to take risks without being overwhelmed or overly fearful. Our relationships with others will be satisfactory and will be in our own best interests, as well as theirs. We will feel worthy and our endeavors will be worthwhile; we will be comfortable in our world and will feel unafraid and kindly towards our fellow man. We will fulfill the old adage of first loving and being kind to ourselves so that we, in turn, can be loving and kind to others. A healthy feeling of self-worth is tantamount to successful living.

The second condition for a happy, healthy life is a sense of security. We cannot afford to have a fear of impending doom, nor a feeling that we might lose everything we have tomorrow. We must then feel secure in our lives if our lives are to operate successfully. You and I must feel, for instance, that our jobs are secure, that we are not going to lose them tomorrow. But more than that, we must know that even if we were to lose our job, we could get one as good or better, in spite of economic or any other circumstances. A feeling of security leads to what is often called peace of mind. We must have a freedom from fear of losing what we have if we are to be comfortable with ourselves and others. It also allows us the freedom to risk and grow because we are not always concentrating on holding onto people, places, and things. This is not to say we do not form attachments, but that we are not hindered by fear of losing them. The greatest security comes, of course, from knowledge that there is a power within us that we can rely on, and that we can always use this power through the law of cause and effect.

Third, if we are to be happy and successful, we need to have a healthy set of expectations. This is sometimes called ambition. Human beings are growth-oriented, goal-oriented organisms. The mind is a problem-solving or goal-getting device. This is what it knows how to do best, and is what it does best. For instance, if the problem is for me to write my name, the goal may be to pick up my pen and put it to paper. The mind gives instructions and carries out the solution to the problem and reaches the selected goal automatically. Conscious and subconscious mind work together in this manner in all areas of our lives. If, however, we do not give the mind direction and do not have a specific goal to be reached, the mind becomes confused, and when this happens, confusion is the result produced in our lives.

We need to have a set of goals, long-term and short-term, that are satisfactory to us, and that we feel relatively sure of attaining. Then our mind will be functioning in the proper manner, seeking ways to fulfill our goals. If we have the proper set of goals our problems are less apt to become overwhelming, and will automatically be resolved as our mind produces the goal fulfillment for us.

Finally, if we are to be fulfilled, we need to have good relationships with others. We need to have a group of acquaintances, large or small, to whom we give something and from whom we get something. Human beings are social organisms and they must have interaction with others of their kind. A fully satisfying life requires friendship and love. It requires meaningful interaction with others. We need to be able to communicate, give and gain support from our peers, without becoming dependent on them or they becoming overly dependent on us. Healthy relationships are a must for a happy, full lifestyle.

If all four of the above mentioned areas—self-worth, ambition, security, relationships—are intact, we will feel very good indeed, and we will be successful in this game of life. However, if one or more of these areas are not up to par, then we begin to suffer the consequences; and the consequences impact negatively on our belief systems which, in turn, produce negative results in our lives.

Having identified the conditions necessary for a healthy mind, body, and life, we need to consider the things that cause damage to those areas of health.

DEALING WITH DISRUPTIVE EMOTIONS

There are four general sets of emotions that can and do cause serious disruption to the four areas we have mentioned as being necessary for a happy, healthy outlook on life.

The first is anger. Anger held onto for any length of time causes serious damage to our self-worth, security, ambition, and personal relations. Anger held onto for too long after the producing incident is often called resentment. Resentment means re-feeling. Re-feeling anger or irritation reinforces negative or faulty belief systems and rapidly becomes generalized. If we are angry at one particular person, we will see that anger begin to express itself in other facets of our lives. Often the anger will leave us with a feeling of low level irritation, and we will respond with anger, or "blowing up," in circumstances that would appear to be quite neutral under ordinary conditions. Also, anger often causes us to relinquish our power to others. If I am angry at someone today, and I do not want to be around that person, I have given that person power over where I go today. And if I stay awake tonight stewing and fretting over what a bad person he or she is, I now have given that person power over how I think and feel. I have even given him or her power over whether I sleep or not. That is far too much power to give another person, but we give this kind of power away much more often than we like to believe.

The second emotion that is terribly destructive is fear. If we stay in fear for very long, we will begin to experience the adverse results, first on a feelings level, and then through adversity and confusion which will appear in our lives. We have all heard of the "fight or flight" syndrome. However, we often forget the implications that anger and fear have for us. When we are confronted with a situation that causes anger or fear, and anger and fear are the normal and necessary responses at the time, our bodies begin immediately to react. Adrenaline begins to flow, heartbeat and respiration speed up, our digestive system shuts down, we are ready for action. This is as it should be. If, however, after the anger or fear producing incident is over, we continue to hold onto the anger or fear, our bodies continue to be in the ready-for-action state, and soon this causes bodily damage. It is as if we sat at a stop sign and kept the accelerator of our automobile pressed to the floor. The bodily motor is racing, so to speak, when we are in anger or fear. Physical problems are often the result of keeping the mind and body in this state of action, when action is no longer necessary. Ulcers, high blood pressure, low back pain, heart problems, are some of the bodily disruptions we can produce by staying in anger and fear. In addition, a state of nervous tension is produced and maintained, causing us to be overly sensitive and often producing anxiety, stress, and depression. The final result will be that of reinforcing faulty belief systems and producing confusion and limitation in our lives. Belief systems based on anger or fear can only produce negative results because they are subtly destroying the positive conditions of self-worth, security, ambition and relationships, which, in turn, reinforces negative belief systems.

There is another kind of fear that we all experience to a larger or lesser degree. It is what we call worry. Worry is the third debilitating emotion that causes problems in our lives. We need to discuss worry as a separate entity, because although it is subtle and may not feel like fear as such, it is just as corrosive in its own way. The dictionary defines worry as "tormenting oneself with disturbing thoughts." I believe torment is the appropriate word for worry. We may be fearful about going to the dentist, or that we are going to lose our job. That is destructive enough, but if we then begin to ruminate about the fear, dredging up all the contingencies surrounding it, we then reinforce the fear and continue to undermine our belief systems. If we continue to worry long enough and hard enough, we will quite often produce the very results that we fear. If we do not produce those results, as we often find the thing we feared or worried about never happens, we are still undermining the things we need for a happy, healthy set of belief systems. Worry leads to confusion and inaction. Procrastination and fatigue are often direct results of the worry syndrome. Also, while our bodies may not react as violently to worry as they do to fear and anger, they are still reacting on a more subtle level and the end result can be just as distressing.

The fourth emotion that undermines happy, healthy living is guilt. Guilt is accepting responsibility for some wrongdoing, either real or imagined. Let me say at this point that time spent feeling guilty is time wasted, and is time spent in an incredibly destructive manner. Guilt is absolutely and unequivocably of no use to anyone. Fear, when reasonable, serves us well. We need to fear a burning building so we can take appropriate action to get ourselves to safety. But we do not need guilt.

I stress this point because so often guilt is equated with piety and so-called goodness. Guilt is, however, a totally irresponsible and inhibiting emotion. Guilt assumes perfection rather than progress. It does not allow for normal human mistakes, and therefore inhibits risk-taking, which is absolutely necessary for growth. An athlete on his or her way to becoming champion may lose several times along the way. If he or she then sits around feeling guilty for the mistakes made, they will never become champions. The thing to do is to learn from the mistakes so one can become a better player. It is the same in the game of life. Of course, guilt often goes further than this. We place labels of good or evil on the outcome of our actions and then torment ourselves with the resultant guilt feelings. We may also give power to others and allow them to make us feel guilty. Many people have become experts in getting what they want by making others feel guilty.

If we have caused harm to another, we need to correct the harm if possible, or at least acknowledge the fact and make our apologies. This is the reasonable, responsible thing to do. But we do not need to feel guilty. In fact, guilt usually impedes the taking of responsible action. There is no way to be happy and healthy and to be into guilt at the same time. Guilt undermines positive belief systems just as effectively as the aforementioned negative emotions, and the negative results show up in our physical health, our feelings, and our lives.

What we have said here is, if we wish to change and expand our belief systems and thereby produce more positive results in our lives, we must first have a healthy sense of self-esteem, security, ambition, and healthy relationships. However, anger, fear, worry, and guilt will cause the above areas to be less than healthy. And here we need to be honest with ourselves. The temptation is to say, "I am, or I am supposed to be, a positive, responsible person, and I have no anger, fear, worry, or guilt." If that is truly the case, then we can begin immediately evaluating and changing our belief systems. But if, as is the case with most of us, we have some negative emotions, then something needs to be done about them. We may find that we seldom allow ourselves to express anger, but when we look closely, we find there is some anger or resentment there nonetheless. Or we may find that while we seldom feel guilt, we are sometimes into worry. We should not apply labels such as good or bad, weak or strong, pious or evil, in evaluating whether or not we have anger, fear, worry, or guilt that needs to be dealt with. We need to be as objective as possible.

IDENTIFYING NEGATIVE REINFORCERS

If we want to identify the anger, fear, worry, and guilt and how it is damaging our self-esteem, security, ambition, and relationships; and further, if we then wish to get rid of these negative emotions, how best can we go about doing it? There are many methods for dealing with this problem. I have chosen to describe the system used by the successful self-help group, Alcoholics Anonymous. This is in no way inferring that anyone reading this book has a problem with alcohol. The choice was made because in the book entitled Alcoholics Anonymous (page 65, 1981 edition), there is a description of an inventory process for identifying how negative emotions undermine areas of health that is as good as any I have come across. Therefore, with their permission, I have adapted their inventory process to meet the needs of a more general population.

Using this adaptation, we will be able to identify and get rid of negative emotions that are reinforcing limited belief systems. Then, using a similar system, we will be able to identify limited belief systems and replace them with belief systems that work.

We will begin by identifying anger. The reason we begin with anger is that it is the easiest emotion to identify. We may have some trouble knowing whether or not we are worried, but we know with whom we are, or have been angry. We need to take a piece of paper and make a list of people with whom we are, or with whom we have been angry. If we can find none, or very little anger, we need to write down on our list those with whom we are, or have been irritated or upset. If we are sure that anger or irritation from the past is completely removed, and we have no feeling of animosity towards that person, then we needn't put that name down. We also need to add our own name to the bottom of the list. When we have completed the list of people, we add more general things that make us angry, irritable, or upset. These would be things like men, women, political parties, income taxes, a certain company, drivers on the freeway, or simply things people as a class do to cause disruption in our lives.

When you have completed your list, take the first name from your list and place it in the left-hand column of a sheet of paper that you have marked off in a manner similar to the example below. The best way to do this is to get some legal size paper and turn it sideways, so you will have room enough for all of the information.

NAME OF: PERSON, PLACE or THING	WHAT THEY DID (DO):	THREATENED MY: —SELF-WORTH —SECURITY —AMBITION (EXPECTATIONS) —RELATIONSHIPS	WHAT DO (DID) I DO? DO (DID) I EXPERIENCE: FEAR, WORRY OR GUILT?

When you have the person's name listed in the left-hand column, then in the second column, write down all of the things that person does or did to make you angry or upset. List those one under the other. Then in the third column, for each item listed in the second column, ask yourself which areas of your life that threatened: self-worth, security, ambition, or your relationships. It may have threatened or affected one area, or it may have affected two, three, or all of the areas, depending on how significant that person was or is in your life. In the fourth column you need to do two things. First, write down what you did, or do, as a result of the things that make you angry in the second column. For instance, if in the second column you wrote down that so-and-so undermined you with the boss, then in the fourth column you write down what you did, or do, as a result. It may be that you gossiped about so-and-so, or you argued with them, or you just went off and pouted. The second thing to do in the fourth column is to write down whether or not the items that so-and-so did in the second column caused you fear, worry, or guilt. If you feel you were, or are, into one or more of these, write the word(s) fear, worry, or guilt in the fourth column. If you feel none of these apply, then, of course, you do not put them down. You might also want to write down a few words about how the fear, worry, or guilt expresses itself in your life. Follow this format for every person, place, or thing from your original list.

If you are honest and objective with your list, you will begin to see two interesting patterns emerge.

First, you will be able to see that when so-and-so does those things in the second column, you do or feel whatever it is you have written in the fourth column. Then you will be able to see that whenever anyone does this in the second column, you do this in the fourth column. That makes you a button waiting to be pushed. Any Tom, Dick, or Harry, whether you know him or not, can get this fourth column response, simply by doing the thing listed in the second column. That is by far too much power to be giving away; however, if you are letting others make you angry, fearful, worried, or guilty, you are in fact giving them power to which they are not entitled.

The second fact that should appear on our inventory list is that we are rapidly running into choices. We can have the anger, fear, worry, and guilt, or we can be healthy and happy in the areas of self-worth, security, ambition, and relationships; but, we cannot have both. Our minds and the universal laws of cause and effect do not work that way. If we choose to hold onto anger, justifiable or not, we must then suffer in the areas we need to be a happy, healthy individual. Forgiving our enemies, or at least letting go of the anger against them, becomes a very practical matter. It is no longer a matter of being the nice thing to do—it becomes a practical necessity if we are to make positive changes in our lives—because it is necessary to do that to be a happy, healthy individual.

Many people, however, would rather get even than get what they want. They say, "I can never forgive old so-and-so for what he or she did to me. It was too terrible." And we might agree that the event described was pretty horrendous. Nonetheless, if the anger is held onto, the individual must suffer in the very areas he or she needs to be happy, healthy, and successful. The anger will affect or cause damage to belief systems that will in turn produce unsatisfactory results in the individual's life. Thus, if we are going to change and expand our belief systems in a positive way, we are going to have to become willing to let go of anger, fear, worry, and guilt. Any satisfaction we would derive from holding onto these negative feelings is far outweighed by the damage they are causing.

Suppose then that you have been as objective and honest as possible and have completed the inventory. You have seen the things we have mentioned and have drawn the conclusion that the thing to do is to get rid of the anger, fear, worry, and guilt. How can you go about doing that?

First of all, you have already begun the process of getting rid of these negative emotions. The fact that you have written them down on paper in an organized fashion and can clearly see their harmful results is a sizeable step in the right direction. It begins to take the power out of these negative emotions. As long as the anger, fear, worry, and guilt are stored in your mind, they have tremendous power over your feelings and behavior. But when you get them on paper, they become objectified and you can clearly see them for what they are—destructive and petty.

Now if you take your list and you share all four columns with another human being, you will find the negative power further reduced. The reason for this is that in discussing your anger, fear, worry, and guilt with another person, you have moved those destructive emotions further from your head, so to speak, and you can now look at them even more objectively. You have also reinforced your decisions to be honest about what is really damaging and limiting your belief systems by getting honest with someone else.

We need to talk for a moment about the person you should choose to share your list. It should be someone you can trust to be discreet and who will keep the information confidential. It need not be a professional counselor, a friend will do. You are not looking for a great deal of feedback. You are not going into analysis. Actually, you will be almost gossiping for the last time. You do not want someone who will reinforce the negativity by supporting your anger and fear, instead of supporting your releasing those negative emotions. You do not want someone saying, "Oh, you are absolutely right. I cannot stand so-and-so either." You simply want someone who will keep an open mind and who understands that you are getting ready to release this negativity—not hold onto it. Also you do not want to pick someone who is going to be critical of you, but one who supports you in what you are doing. If you feel you have no one like that in your life, you may want to ask a minister or priest to hear your inventory. Remember, however, that you are not doing confession of sins, but merely presenting facts. You may even go to a counselor if you choose. However, if you do not have at least one trusted friend in your life, it is time you found one. Friends are not hard to find—we only think they are. We simply need to begin being friendly, and we will be surprised at the results. In almost every community, there are what are termed "new thought" churches and groups. They often follow the ideals we have been expressing, and all of them are committed to positive thinking and improving lifestyles. These places are ideal for making friends who will support you in your endeavors.

At any rate, you will need to share your list with someone, and when you do that, you will have taken considerable power out of the negatives on your list. The fact that you have organized your thoughts and put them on paper and then shared them with another has moved the thoughts away from you to the extent that they will no longer be exercising such a strong hold over you, and you will become much more willing to let them go.

Immediately following the sharing of your list with another person, you return home and simply ask the universal power within to remove the anger, fear, worry, and guilt. And if you are the least bit willing, that is exactly what will happen. The negative emotions will begin to disappear, and when that happens, your self-worth, security, ambition, and relationships automatically begin to heal. A wonderful sense of freedom and confidence will begin to take place within you, and you will begin to feel a sense of happiness and joy. Things that used to bother you will no longer seem important; people, places and things will cease to have the power to push your buttons, and can no longer make you feel angry or sad.

People often ask, what about the subconscious negative attitudes and emotions we cannot remember? This is an interesting question. There was a time when we would work with people, going into subconscious, attempting to uncover subconscious material which was causing them problems. This system was difficult and time consuming. It has been my experience, and the experience of others, that when we ask the inner universal power to remove the negatives which we are consciously aware of, the similar subconscious material is also removed. We know this happens because we no longer respond in the same way when confronted with situations that used to distress us. We do not respond with nearly as much anger, fear, worry, and guilt as previously, and these feelings are quite easily overcome. Therefore, we conclude that the subconscious material has been removed, as well as those things we can consciously remember.

As a final step, you may find it necessary to talk with some of the people on your list, making a simple apology for your own part in the discord that has damaged a relationship or hurt another. By reviewing your list, you will know whether or not you need to make an apology or talk with someone. Remember, however, not to rehash their faults in the process. You are simply getting free of anything that might impede your own progress towards changing and expanding your belief systems.

DEALING WITH LIMITED BELIEF SYSTEMS

Having dealt with the anger, fear, worry, and guilt that have been reinforcing negative or limited belief systems, we then need to address the belief systems themselves. We need to identify and get rid of belief systems that are producing limitation in our lives and replace them with belief systems that produce the results we want. We use a slightly different format here.

In the first column we now list general areas of our life that we would like to see improved or expanded. For instance, if we wish to have more money, a really great romantic relationship, or a successful career, we need to first identify what our present belief systems are in those areas. Thus, in the first column, we write down money, men or women, career, and so on. Then in the second column, we now write down what we really believe about them. For instance, we may believe that money is hard to get. Or we may believe one has to have money to make money, that a person must have education and contacts to obtain wealth, rich people are bad people, money is the root of all evil, we can only make so much money. Whatever we believe about money, we write it down in the second column. Of course, we all have positive as well as limited beliefs concerning money, relationships, career, and health. However, we are only writing down the limited or negative beliefs here, because these are the stumbling blocks that are standing in the way of the realization of our goals. When we identify and get rid of the limited beliefs, the positive will automatically take over.

Finally, we make a third column, and here we write down the results that take place in our lives as a result of the limiting beliefs indicated in the second column. The results may be that we worry about money, we never seem to have enough money, we always attract the wrong people, we talk about how hard it is to pay our bills, and so on.

We continue this process for every area of our lives that we wish to improve. When our list is completed, we will be able to see that if what we believe is being produced in our lives, it is no wonder that we are limiting ourselves. If our last marriage was a disaster and we are still holding onto the resultant hurt and fear, it will undoubtedly affect our present relationships. If we feel men are not to be trusted, or women are incapable of understanding men, then it will be very difficult, if not impossible, for us to have a healthy relationship or marriage.

Whatever we discover on our list, we again share it with another. This will begin to take the power out of the faulty belief systems themselves. And we ask the power within us to remove these limiting and faulty beliefs, along with their results. As the faulty belief systems begin to falter and disappear we will have begun to remove the core of the problems and limitations in our lives. We are no longer holding onto belief systems that produce limitation in our lives, nor are we reinforcing them with negative emotions.

Although the processes described in this chapter require a bit of work on our part, they are by no means as difficult as continuing to struggle with negative belief systems. Do not allow yourself to complicate your inventories or to see them as overwhelming. The process is simple and does not take a great deal of time. If you feel a different format would be better for you, fine; use any format you like to get the information on paper. However, you do need to write it down. The writing of anything clarifies it and allows you to deal with it effectively. Also, do not fear the process. The end result will be that you are free of the very things you fear.

After writing, sharing, and asking for the negatives in our belief systems to be removed, the only thing left to do is the replacement of old limited belief systems with ones that are new and unlimited. These new beliefs will then be produced in our lives. We will see how to accomplish this in the next chapter.

CHAPTER VI
SETTING GOALS AND GETTING GOALS

In the preceding chapter, we discussed the system of identifying and getting rid of what we do not want. Now we need to know how to get what we do want. If we have been conscientious in identifying and releasing our negative belief systems and their reinforcers, they have already been or are in the process of being removed from our conscious and subconscious minds. We begin to feel much better, more confident, and secure. We have taken on a new attitude toward ourselves and the world around us. We are no longer small and everything else big. Now is the time to decide what it is we want and to begin getting it.

Let me mention a word of caution here. If you have done your inventory, shared it with someone, and released the negatives to your inner power, and you do not feel better immediately do not throw up your arms in despair. Some of us have such deep-seated negativity in certain areas of our lives that we have developed a habit of not feeling well or happy. Do not worry about this. Just know that the negative feelings are being removed and go on with your goal setting. If however, you are so depressed or anxious, or if you have become addicted to alcohol or drugs, for instance, then of course you will need to seek professional help or one of the excellent self-help groups, such as Alcoholics or Narcotics Anonymous. Do not hesitate to seek outside help if you feel you need it. The same applies for any physical ailments you may have. This book should then only be used to support any formal support systems that you feel are necessary.

Now that we have identified and dealt with faulty belief systems, we are ready to replace them with something that works. We are now at the point where we can begin to set goals. Setting the proper goals will do more to establish and reinforce positive belief systems than any other single thing we can do. Remember, we said human beings are growth-oriented, goal-oriented organisms; therefore, they must have goals if their lives are to be in accord with natural and spiritual law. In addition, and more important, since our belief systems are going into the subconscious mind and producing results in our lives, we need to establish goals that will give the laws of cause and effect proper direction so that we will produce specific, desired results. This, in turn, will continue to expand our belief systems, which will then produce more and more good in our lives.

Up to now many of our beliefs, expectations, and goals have been based on information gathered from outside sources, which are, in the main, quite limiting. We have listened all too often to what others have had to say concerning what we can expect out of life. We have become so caught up in the appearance of the conditions surrounding us that we have become convinced we are limited and controlled by those conditions. We are now going to change all of that as we go about setting our new goals. We have become secure in the knowledge that our own thoughts and beliefs have, through the laws of cause and effect, attracted the conditions within which we find ourselves. Therefore, if we are to change our conditions, we must boldly change our minds, and when we do this, the conditions of our lives will automatically change. We do this by first setting goals that will give us satisfaction, not what someone else thinks we ought to have or do. This does not mean that we are ignoring or becoming hostile to the people in our lives. Far from it. When we take control of our thoughts and decide what is best for us, our relationship to people and conditions will improve significantly.

At this point, we need to take a piece of paper and write down what we want. Remember, the sky is the limit. You can have it all. There is nothing too farfetched for the universal power, working through the laws of cause and effect, to produce in your life. Be bold. Put down the really big things you have wished for and dreamed about, as well as the little things. What kind of career would you like to have? How much money? What kind of love relationships? Write it all down.

Sometimes when we get to the point of deciding what we really want, we become a bit stuck. We have the feeling we cannot make a proper decision about what we want. We feel we just do not know. If this is a problem for you, there are several things you can do. First, make sure you have released the majority of negative emotions and beliefs on your lists. Sometimes we do know what we want, but are afraid to make a real commitment to having it. We feel it would be too hard to get, or that we do not really deserve it, or that it would be selfish if we were to really be prosperous, for instance. If you are still having difficulty deciding what you want, it may be because you are approaching decision-making in the wrong way. For instance, you do not need to know the exact job or career you would like to have. What you need to know here, and what you might want to put down on paper is what you would love to do for eight hours a day. It does not matter whether you can think of a job where you could be doing that. Just put down what you would really like to do and how much money you would like to make doing it. Remember, the law of cause and effect will attract the actual position to you; and if one doesn't now exist, it will be created for you. Do not allow yourself to slip into limited thinking at this point. Anything you want, you can have.

Another idea may also be of help to you if you are having trouble deciding what it is you want. This is the idea that nothing has to be forever. If you make a decision now and later change your mind, you are not stuck with the original decision. If you change your mind, you simply change or add to your list so that it corresponds to the new desire. In fact, we all change as we grow and gain self-confidence and assurance, and our goals often change in this process. This is as it should be. We should be expanding in all areas of our lives, continually raising our sights above the previous level, and continually experiencing more and greater abundance in our lives.

At any rate, we need to decide what it is we want and put it down on paper. In addition to the large, spectacular goals, we also need to write down some things that will bring joy into our lives on an ongoing basis. These can be simple things—like going to a good movie or play with someone you like; attending a dance, going out to dinner, playing cards with friends, walking in the park, taking up painting, reading a good novel. The list is inexhaustible. Just make sure you write down the things you really want and enjoy, not what you think you ought to enjoy or what others say you should enjoy. We all need some fun in our lives, and we need to begin having it right now.

Once we have our list of wants, goals, and desires complete, we need to have a method by which we can introduce them into the law of cause and effect so they will move through our subconscious mind into the larger subconscious and be produced in our lives.

There are many ways to do this; however, my preference is with the system developed by Dr. Ernest Holmes, in which he coined the phrase, "spiritual mind treatment." Lest that term frighten anyone, we will simply call our system treatment. Or, if you prefer to call it something else, feel free to do so. This is a personal program, and that which works best for you is what you need to be doing. In fact, if you feel more comfortable with another system than the one about to be described, you should use it. You are the best judge of what feels right and will work best for you.

As we discuss this system, you may want to refer back to the chart on page 28 to refresh your memory and clarify the issues. When we speak of treatment, we do not mean doing something to ourselves or others, the way we would think of a nurse or doctor treating a wound. For our purposes we are using the word treatment to denote a system of focusing our thoughts in a certain direction, and reinforcing these thoughts until they become belief systems that will reproduce their exact replicas in our lives and our world. We will discuss a five-step method of doing this, and then you can use that system or adapt it so it will be more to your own liking.

A SYSTEM FOR SETTING GOALS

The first step in our treatment, or the focusing of our attention and directing the law of cause and effect, is called recognition. We are attempting here to recognize or become aware of, a power that is greater than ourselves, but not separate from ourselves. We want to decide what that power is and how it works. Let me say here that we again need to write out all five steps of our treatment. When we write something down, we clarify it in our minds. If you feel there is just too much writing to be done, I can sympathize with you. However the writing gives the process much more power and is often the element of success, and it is not that difficult once we get started.

So, we consider the proposition discussed in the earlier chapters of this book. We come to a decision that we have kept an open mind and are at least willing to consider the possibility of a universal mind, which was first cause of everything in the universe, including us, and that this universal mind and power is not only around us, but also within us. To solidify our thinking on this point, and to make direct connection with this universal mind and power, we need to reinforce our belief systems in this area by writing them down on paper. We need to write down what we believe the universal mind or power to be and how we feel it works.

An example of this would be universal mind is contained in everything; therefore, it is power, abundance, wealth, love, beauty, and so on. And it works through the law of cause and effect, its thoughts being the cause, and the things that are created being the effect. If you feel your higher power has a personality, if you call it God or the great spirit, write that idea down also. I will give an example of a completed written treatment at the end of this chapter, so that you can visualize the format. However, the ideas should be your own. You can write a treatment, one that will be meaningful to you, better than anyone else. It does not have to be long or complicated. It simply needs to be meaningful to you.

The second step in our treatment, or our declaration of intention, is called unification. Once we have decided what universal mind is, we need to connect it in our thinking to ourselves. We do this by writing down how we think the universal mind and power applies to us personally. We need to clarify how we can personally use the larger power in our own lives.

In this step we would write something like this. The universal mind and myself are one. I am part and parcel of the universal mind. Since everything, including me, is created out of universal mind, I am therefore a part of the universal mind. And since I have a conscious mind that is part of universal mind, I am in fact using universal mind and power all of the time. I certainly am not all of universal mind, but I am a part of it, therefore, I must also be power, abundance, beauty, health, energy, and love. In addition to that, my thoughts must create through the law of cause and effect in my own universe the same as the larger mind creates in the larger universe. Finally, since universal mind is within me as well as all around me, I do not have to go anywhere but within my own mind to use the larger power, to get guidance and direction from it, and to expand and give direction to the law of cause and effect for any purpose I may desire.

Again, the ideas mentioned above are only suggested guidelines. You will want to write down how you and universal mind are one in your own words. It must only be meaningful to you. As long as you clarify in your own mind that you and universal mind are not separate entities, but that you are using universal mind every time you think, whether you know it or not, and that you have much more power than you have heretofore used, then you will be on the right track. Some people find it more satisfactory and meaningful to combine the recognition and unification steps. Again, this is up to you.

Also, do not feel that you are giving up your individuality or identity here. What you are stating is that we are all individual expressions of the one universal mind, but we are free to express our identity in any way we choose. We simply want to be able to use more of the power in a more personal and effective way. Finally, we also need to know that if we are all part of universal mind, it follows that we are also one with each other since we all use the same universal mind and power. As I write this book and you read it, we are both using a part of the same universal mind, and are thus, one with each other. I hope I have not confused you here. I do not mean to indicate that you are not a separate, unique, and special individual, because you are. I am simply saying that we are all connected with each other on a much deeper level than we may have previously realized. This fact, that we are all using the universal mind, is what allows us to be able to communicate with each other, to love one another, to join together in common cause, and to have understanding, humor, and a sense of togetherness. At the same time, each individual has a unique wealth of talent and originality to bring to the tapestry of the whole.

Now we come to the part we have all been waiting for. In the third step, which we will call the declaration, we are going to write down what it is we want. This may have seemed to be a long time coming, with all of the preparatory work that has gone on before. However, most people are not realizing their potential precisely because they do not, in one way or another, lay the groundwork for bringing their belief systems in line with what they want to see produced in their lives. If we have been thorough in listing our negative ideas and belief systems, and have released them, we have laid a foundation for new belief systems that will allow us to move forward as never before. We can now put on paper what it is we really want, and can have positive assurance that that is what we can expect to be created in our lives.

We now need to take our list of the things we desire and transfer them to the third step of our treatment. There are two ways to do this. The first is to write out the first two steps, recognition and unification for each declaration we make. Thus, if we were writing treatments for a new career, a love relationship, and improved health, we would write out all five steps for each thing we desired. Steps one and two would then relate closely to the third, or declaration step, and would reinforce our belief systems concerning the universal mind and our relationship to it, which is the basis for believing the law of cause and effect will produce what we want in our lives.

The second way we can write our treatments is to write a general statement for steps one and two, and then put several desires in the third step declaration. Although this is a more expeditious method and requires less writing, the first two steps are less specific and usually do not reinforce our belief systems as well as when we write out all of the steps for each thing we desire. This is especially true when we are just beginning to experiment with goal setting and treatment. Remember, we are not held to any hard and fast process, and the systems discussed in this book should be adapted to fit individual needs.

One way or another, we need to take our list of wants and put them in our treatment. Suppose, however, that when you look at your original lists of wants and desires you find that you have listed twenty, or forty, or seventy things that you want. How can you handle that many things? There is nothing wrong with wanting that many things, and it is better than not allowing yourself to decide what you want, but it does sometimes become unwieldly and confusing. If our list is quite long, we probably need to pare it down to a workable size, at least to begin with. We might review our list and see if some of the things we are wanting are quite similar to others, and therefore can be combined. Another thing we can do is to prioritize our list. Which of the wants and needs do we consider to be of paramount importance, and which are of lesser importance?

This brings up an important point that applies throughout our attempt to have what we want produced in our lives. We have said there is a great deal of difference between "I would like to have," and "I really want." To direct the law of cause and effect successfully, we need to change liking to have into a want and then into a strong desire, a magnificent obsession, if you can accept that term in its most positive sense. If we do not do this, our thoughts and beliefs will too easily be distracted and we will not be giving consistent direction to the universal subconscious mind, which in turn, will not be able to determine what we wish to have produced. The final result will not be what we want; or the result will be only partially successful. Therefore, we want to draw from our list those items to which we are most strongly committed.

The best procedure, to begin with, is to pick the two or three desires or needs that you want the most—the really big things, and one or two of the ongoing smaller things that will put some fun in your life right now. Later, more can be added. It is also a good idea to make one of the things you are treating for, a personal improvement goal. This may be something on strengthening positive belief systems, or for a better understanding of spiritual power, more self-confidence, or anything you feel you would like to see happening inside of yourself. The reason for this is obvious. We have gotten rid of the negative belief systems through the inventory procedure and now we want to replace them with positive belief systems. This automatically makes us feel more secure and confident about ourselves and strengthens our conviction that there really is a power in the universe that we can, and are, using to realize all of the good we can accept. This type of treatment will, in turn, strengthen our request for specific things we want to see created in our outer world.

When we have decided what we want, we write it down in the third step of our treatment, the declaration step. And it is most important that we write it in the present tense, as if we have already received it. We do not say we are going to receive it at some future date, but rather that we have it right now. You may be feeling that this does not make much sense. Here we are, with a pile of bills and no money in the bank, and we are saying we have all the prosperity we could want. Is that not trying to fool ourselves? What good will that possibly do?

The reason we write down that we already have what we desire is not to try to fool ourselves or anyone else, nor is it to deny present conditions. If we are broke at the present moment, or lonely, or out of a job, that is the reality of the situation and we are not pretending it is some other way. That would be foolish. To deny the reality of our problems would be very much like the story of the three men who had died and found themselves in the "hot place," usually designated as hell. As they were sitting there amongst the raging fires, they began discussing their demise. When the first man was asked how he happened to be in the hot place, he stated that he was of the Catholic faith and women had been his weakness. The second man, when questioned, stated that he was Jewish and ham sandwiches had been his weakness. They then turned to the third man who was sitting with his eyes closed and perspiration running down his face, and asked him how he came to be in the hot place. Without opening his eyes, the third man stated, 'I am an advocate of spiritual mind treatment. It is not hot, and I am not here."

We do not want to fall into the trap of ignoring present problems. Then, why would we write down a treatment that contained the solution to our problems as if that had already happened? Is that not denying the present problems? If we put our problems and their solutions in the proper perspective, this confusion should resolve itself. In the first place, our problems are in our lives because of faulty belief systems, which operating through the subconscious law of cause and effect produced undesirable conditions for us. Now that we have changed those belief systems to positive, we can expect new results to be created in our lives, regardless of what the present circumstances appear to be. Therefore, we can be assured that whatever we are writing down is immediately taken up by our subconscious mind, placed into the larger subconscious law and is already producing the right results. It is sort of like the situation where someone calls you up and says that your old Uncle Ned died and left you a million dollars. The will, of course, would have to be probated and there would be a short period of time to lapse before you would actually receive the money, but the money is yours. You may not yet have the physical currency in your hand, or in your bank, but it is yours.

This then is the feeling we want to generate in writing our treatment. As soon as we put it on paper, the law of cause and effect goes into action, attracting or creating the things we desire. Therefore, for all intents and purposes we already have them, even if they are not yet in our hands. There is also an important scientific reason for stating you already have the things you desire. The subconscious mind does not, in fact cannot, differentiate between the thought and the things. Nor does, or can, the subconscious mind, which operates on the law of cause and effect, make this distinction. That is to say, whatever we give the subconscious mind, from our conscious mind's belief system, will end up being produced in our lives in precisely the manner we have given it. Thus, if we tell the subconscious we are going to have it at some future time, the subconscious will wait for a future time to place our desire into the law of cause and effect. However, if we state or write down that we have it now, the subconscious will begin working on our declaration to that effect immediately. The important thing then, is to always work in the present tense when declaring what we want to see produced in our lives, and not to let present problems or circumstances deter us. We created limited circumstances for ourselves by improper use of the law; now we are going to change our directions to the law, and new unlimited conditions will be the result, beginning right now.

I hope I have not made a simple process confusing. I just want to make sure that I cover the common questions that have come up in the past when I have presented these ideas. All we are actually saying here is that in the third step declaration, we declare that we already have whatever it is we may want. The declaration might say something like, "I have the perfect job, making X amount of money. This job gives me great satisfaction. I work with friendly people, travel extensively, and utilize my talents to their fullest. My employers appreciate me and my work, and tell me so. I look forward to going to work every morning. My job and my salary give me the prestige I desire."

You will need to decide how to write a statement that best describes what you want, and then write it down as if you already have it. That is all there is to it. The written statement can be as long or as short as you want it to be. The main consideration in writing treatments is that they be meaningful to you.

If you decide to write more than one declaration,

more than one thing you want on a single treatment, rather than writing out all of the steps for each desired thing, you would write steps one and two, recognition and unification, on a separate sheet of paper, and then use additional sheets to write your declarations, and finally writing steps four and five on the last sheet.

Step four in our treatment, or our goal setting and getting process, is thanksgiving. This is an optional step. Many people feel that giving thanks smacks of religion or old-fashioned prayer, in which a higher power is separate from the individual. They say that giving thanks reinforces the idea of separateness and sabotages the belief that the universal power and we are one, and that it also inhibits the belief that the power resides within each of us. They also state you only need to declare your word and believe, and the thing you want will be produced through the law of cause and effect; therefore, you are actually directing the higher power within, and since it is part and parcel with you, you would only be thanking yourself.

These arguments are not without validity and you should take them into consideration when deciding whether or not this step will be helpful to you. It is my opinion, and surely only an opinion, that the detriment of possibly increasing the feeling of separateness from the inner universal power is outweighed by the advantages of writing down a sentence or two of thanks. For me this step has a tendency to reinforce the belief system that I already have what I have declared in the third step, even if I do not see it physically at this time. The reasoning behind this idea is that if someone told me a million dollars had been left to me, and that it would shortly be in my hands, I would surely say thank you very much. Also, if I am only thanking myself when I thank the universal power within, that's O.K., too. We need to start treating ourselves with the same consideration we afford to others. Finally, many of us have special belief systems about a higher power or God. Although we feel this power is contained within us, it is also all around us, and is infinitely larger than our own limited power, therefore it makes some sense to us to thank the universal power for delivering the goods, even though we are not separate from that power and go within our selves to contact it.

If you choose to use the fourth step, thanksgiving, you can say thank you for having already received that which you have declared to be yours in step three. Some of us also say thanks to the universal power or first cause for setting up a system whereby we can learn how to use the laws of cause and effect for the purpose of having whatever good we wish created in our lives. Usually, three or four written sentences will cover the fourth step.

The final, and possibly most significant step is called release. This step is the culmination of our treatment, because it is in this step that we will attempt to release our declaration into the subconscious laws of cause and effect so that it can be produced in our internal or external world. This is the step that causes us to remember that we are not the ones who will have to make the desired result come about; rather, the larger universal mind within and without, will through spiritual and natural law immediately begin creating the necessary conditions by which our goal will be produced.

If we write out a treatment, meditate upon it every morning and then frantically run around trying to make it happen, we will be more apt to interfere with the universal laws than to assist them. We have mentioned giving a problem to a computer to solve for us and then trying to figure the result ourselves. That would be foolish, and it would certainly not be the proper use of our computer. The same holds true of the treatment process. We no longer need to do the work of the universal computer by pushing, pulling, or manipulating eternal circumstances. Instead, we will remember that our belief systems caused us to be in the circumstances in which we find ourselves, and since we have changed our belief systems and know how the laws of cause and effect work, we will allow those laws to change our circumstances and produce our goals. All we need to do is to write our treatment, release it, and to quietly pay attention to what is happening within and around us.

Of course, we are not going to forget all about our goal, but neither are we going to hold onto it in our thoughts and by doing so, attempt to force it to happen by thinking about it harder or rushing around trying to make something happen. If we attempt to do either of these activities, we will stand a good chance of missing guidance and direction, as well as the answers themselves when they appear.

We need to do two things with our treatment after releasing it to the laws of cause and effect. First, we need to spend ten or fifteen minutes in the morning, and the same amount of time in the evening meditating and reading over our treatments. We need to have our ideas of recognition, and the unification of ourselves with universal mind firmly implanted in our minds. We need to be sure of our declaration every day, and we need to know it has already been released to the universal power and laws. You may ask here, if the treatment has been released, why do we need to keep going over it? Does not that act show we do not believe we already have it? The answer is, yes, we have already released our declaration into the law of cause and effect, and if our conscious belief system is at a high enough level, we will see it produced immediately. However, as has been mentioned, most of us are working with new belief systems, or at least we are expanding positive belief systems. We must then continue to reinforce these belief systems daily, or we will begin to doubt or negate our treatments, especially when our circumstances appear not to be changing. We are daily reinforcing our treatment so we will not inadvertantly divert the laws of cause and effect into another direction by changing our minds, or by letting negative appearing circumstances weaken our belief systems. We will talk more on this matter of release and meditation in a later chapter.

The second thing we need to do with our treatment after releasing it is to go about our business of the day as usual, but with one important new endeavor. We will pay attention to what is going on around us, as well as listening for intuitive thoughts that will lead us towards our goal. When we receive a thought that seems to direct us to do a certain thing in the direction of the desired goal, we will do that thing. If someone says something that appears to have to do with our goal, we will follow that up also. Taking action in this manner, calmly and confidently, will lead us to our goal, attract it to us, or create it for us, in an amazingly short period of time.

Some people ask at this point, "What if I follow a course of action suggested by an intuitive thought, another person, or something I see, hear, or read, and it turns out to be wrong? How will I know the right things to do so I will not make a mistake?" The answer is: you cannot make a mistake. If you choose as wisely as you are able, everything that you do after you have written and released your treatment will be leading toward your stated goal, unless you change your belief system regarding that particular goal. If you take a path that is not in conjunction with your stated goal, you will be rapidly shown that you are off the track and you can put yourself right again. For instance, if your treatment is for a job with particular properties that will give you fulfillment and an excellent salary, you will not be offered a lesser job, or if you are, you will know not to take it. As long as you keep your goal firmly fixed in your mind, then you will only receive that which corresponds precisely with your goal.

In the release step, one might write down a statement, such as, "I now release this treatment to the law of cause and effect, knowing that my stated desire is already mine. I am being drawn to it, and it to me. I totally believe this is the way things work for me and I know my word will not return to me void."

The thing to do now, is to take a piece of paper, and from your list of wants and desires pick two or three, and write out a treatment using the previously described five steps of recognition, unification, declaration, thanksgiving, and release. Then, read your treatment every day, reaffirming it in your mind, releasing it to the laws of cause and effect, and finally paying attention and taking appropriate action with the full knowledge that that which you desire is already yours.

The treatment shown below is simply an example. You may decide to use this format, or another more suited to you personally.

An example treatment might look something like this:

I. Recognition of Universal Mind

There is a power in the universe that is greater than I am, and I can use it. This power is in, through, and around everything. It is prosperity, success, energy, health, and love. It works through natural and spiritual laws, one of which is the law of cause and effect.

II. Unification With Universal Mind

Since universal mind is in everything it is also in me. My mind is a use of that mind and my thoughts are always creating. The thoughts I have now are creating now, because of my connection with the universal mind and the laws of cause and effect.

III. Declaration

I now have abundance and prosperity. It comes to me from the universal source, of which I am a part. I have more than enough money to do whatever I want, whenever I want. I am financially independent.

IV. Thanksgiving

I give thanks for my abundance and prosperity, and for the knowledge of how to use the laws of cause and effect.

V. Release

I now release this treatment to the universal laws of cause and effect, knowing that it is being produced in my life now.

CHAPTER VII
TAKING ACTION AND ENJOYING THE PROCESS

Now that we have rid ourselves of faulty belief systems and begun to replace them with positive and less limited goals and objectives by writing them in treatment form, what do we do? What is the appropriate action to take towards realizing our goal?

In earlier chapters, we discussed some general ideas on the proper kinds of action to be taken in expediting the realization of our goals. We said we did not want to write a treatment concerning our goals, release it to the subconscious law of cause and effect, and then start running around trying to do the work of the universal subconscious ourselves. We need to remember that the law of cause and effect will create the desired results, therefore, any action we take must be in conjunction with that law. At the same time, we cannot expect to sit at home and do nothing at all. So what do we need to do?

All of our action must be activity that reinforces the belief that our desires are being produced in our lives, beginning right now. And, in fact, the most significant activity will be done at home. We need to set aside ten or fifteen minutes in the morning and in the evening just before retiring for meditation and treatment work. We will call this meditation with a purpose. There are infinite numbers of ways to meditate. However, we do not need to go into exhaustive research on the intricacies of meditation. For our purposes, a simple and direct approach will do quite well.

The key to all meditation is to become as relaxed as possible. However, we do not want to become so relaxed we go to sleep. When people begin to meditate, one of two things usually happens: they go to sleep, or their head attacks them. Dozens of unrelated thoughts seem to race through their minds. A good way of overcoming this problem is to read a few paragraphs out of a book that you find helpful or quieting. In fact, this is an excellent practice for beginning a period of meditation, no matter how you find yourself responding to meditation. Deep breathing, tensing and relaxing your muscles, saying a meaningless word over and over, are also ways in which you can help yourself to relax. There are many good books on relaxation techniques and meditation to be found in most bookstores. It is also a very good idea to read a few pages from a book that is particularly inspirational or uplifting to you during this meditation time.

Once you have become sufficiently relaxed, you will want to begin your treatment work. Spend some time considering the first two steps of your treatment. Can you believe the ideas you have written? Consider the universal creative energy and attempt to become connected with it. Begin to know that the power is in and around you, and that you can use it.

Then consider step three, the declaration of your desire. Know that it is now coming into your life and that it is now true for you. Give thanks and release your treatment into the universal subconscious, knowing that it is already yours.

Now, repeating what we said in an earlier chapter, we go out into the world, paying attention to what is going on around us. We have placed our desires into the universal law of cause and effect, therefore, the thing is already being produced for us. Everything we are doing from this point on is, in effect, leading us to our goal. We need to be alert to signs that point us in the right direction. And they will come. We also need to listen for intuitive thoughts and ideas that will come to us, also indicating the direction we should take. Everything is taking place that needs to take place for the realization of our goal. We need to work with ourselves until we know and believe that the thing we desire is already ours, that we are in fact, that thing. If our goal is the right career, we know that the position we now have is a stepping stone to that career. If we desire the right romantic relationship, we know that all of the relationships we now have, romantic or otherwise, are preparing us for that right relationship.

If, during the day, we get pulled into circumstances that appear negative and seem to pull us down and cause us doubts and frustration, we need to take a few minutes to reaffirm our goals and know that this situation is only temporary. We are being true to our vision, we know the goal is already ours. We need to do this with a light touch, so to speak. We need to keep in mind that we are not trying to force anything to happen, rather, we are letting it happen through the law of cause and effect. If we maintain our belief system, then nothing but the desired result can happen. It is simply done unto us as we believe.

Of course, we will also take any active action that seems appropriate. If we are treating for the right career, we might want to peruse the newspaper want ads and if anything catches our attention we will follow up on that lead. We might also talk to people who are already established in a field similar to that which we are seeking. If we think certain people would be helpful in giving us direction or help in realizing our goals, we will talk with them also. Soon we will begin to see a pattern and a sense of direction begin to emerge, and when we follow it, our goal will suddenly appear. Then we come to know that we can have it all.

At this point, we need to reexamine an earlier question. Suppose we take the wrong action. Suppose we apply for a job that we believe to be the right job, and it turns out not to be what we expected? Suppose we fall in love with someone who appears to be the perfect mate, and then later turns out not to be the right person at all? If you have established your goal and your vision, it will be impossible for the wrong thing to be demonstrated in your life. If the job or the relationship is not in line with your goal you will not get the job, or you will not be able to make the relationship permanent, no matter how hard you try. Remember, we are working with a law, and laws do not change; therefore, if we remain steadfast in desiring our goal, what we have written down as our goal will be produced in our lives, and nothing else can be produced.

If you apply for a job that looks perfectly in line with your desires and you are turned down, it is because something in that job is not in line with what you want. If you fall in love with someone and they are not willing to make a commitment, it is because that is not the right partner for you. These experiences are in fact preparing you for the final acceptance of your goal. Remember, you are not going to settle for second best.

The aforementioned ideas are most important, because unless we understand that it is impossible to end up with the wrong results, we too often get discouraged when things appear not to be working out. So if we know, and we must know this, that everything is leading towards the expression of our goal, we will not get caught up in present circumstances nor will we give up at the crucial point, just when our goal is about to be realized.

Our way of thinking about action or activity will be different from what it has been in the past. The first action we need to take is to follow the steps outlined in this book. We will make our lists, share them with another, and get rid of both our limited belief systems and their reinforcers. Then we write down our goals in the manner previously described. Finally, every morning and evening, we meditate on our goals, knowing that through the universal laws of cause and effect, we already have them "in mind," therefore, we already have them "in fact."

We move out into our world almost as an objective viewer, a scientist, testing our hypothesis. We are already feeling more self-confident, more secure, more ambitious, because we have gotten rid of the negative belief systems and replaced them with positive exciting goals. We are no longer victims of our circumstances, rather, we now know that the circumstances were produced by our past thinking, and our new thinking will produce new circumstances in our lives.

Our activity now has a purpose, our goals are in place, and we are approaching life in a new way. We have a theoretical basis for limitless opportunities. Now we are going to test the theory and watch it become reality. In our meditation we have opened the channels to the universal mind; therefore, we are getting guidance and direction from that larger mind that is within us, and which knows precisely what to do to reach our goals. We take time to listen to our inner voice, which will be the larger mind giving us intuitive thoughts concerning the proper action we are to take. This may seem uncomfortable or strange at first, but soon we will begin to get thoughts that say, go here, or do that, and when we follow that direction we find it was precisely the right thing to do. Thus, we begin to trust our intuitive thoughts more and more.

In addition, we are looking at the people, places and things that surround us in a new way. Since all of our activity is leading to our goals, we will be looking and listening for those things or words that, in addition to our intuitive thoughts, indicate a direction to take towards the realization of our goals.

However, we do not want to discuss our goals with everyone we meet. If we do, we will find that many of our acquaintances are either skeptical or incredulous. Their first reaction will be, it cannot be done. Or they may even feel we have become quite strange indeed. This will have a tendency to weaken our position and to inhibit the objective testing of the theory. You will want to discuss your innermost desires and goals only with those people who you know will understand and support you. If you do not have anyone like that in your life, do not worry, you soon will have. Until then, it is better to keep your goals to yourself. Remember, you are not alone. Universal mind is working through you, and the laws of cause and effect are in operation whether or not you are discussing them.

At the same time, although you are only discussing your actual goals with a select few, you are seeing and listening to what is going on around you. Very rapidly, you will begin to hear someone say something that backs up your intuitive thoughts, and when you follow that direction, you find it is also leading toward your goal. Some people believe that their spiritual world is one thing and the material world is something else, that they are somehow separate entities. They feel that they must be removed from the real world to be spiritual. According to our theory, this cannot be so. The so-called spiritual world and the physical world are simply two sides of the same coin. In fact, they are one in the same thing. Thought takes place in the realm of the unseen or spirit, but it always results in something being produced in the physical world. This is the basis of life, and it is how the world works.

So, if we hear someone say, "So-and-so is talking about starting a certain type of business," and it appears to be in line with one of our goals, it behooves us to give so-and-so a call and maybe invite them to lunch, or at least indicate our interest in knowing more about their venture. If we run across something in our reading that has to do with our goals, we follow that up. These things are as much guidance from the universal mind as are intuitive thoughts. And if we are truly testing our hypothesis, that universal mind is working through us by means of the law of cause and effect to bring about and produce our goals, then we need to follow all leads, whether they be from our inner power or in our material world.

We want to avoid thinking of spiritual, or mental, as removed from our material world. In fact, Ernest Holmes, the founder of Science of Mind, stated that if you want to find out how spiritual someone is, look at his or her physical and material surroundings. They are a good indication of the inner person, because they have been created out of the way that person thinks. This is not to say we have to be millionaires to be spiritual. Neither, however, ought we be suffering paupers. Deprivation and suffering are not spiritual, nor are they the result of proper use of the spiritual law of cause and effect. Abundance, prosperity, health, and love are the results of proper use of the law.

At any rate, we will pay attention to those things that are going on in our daily activities, and when they indicate something to be done towards the realization of our goal, we will follow up. We want to avoid the situation that befell the man in a little story I heard the other day. It seems the man found himself in the middle of a torrential rain that was causing the river to overflow and begin flooding the town. The water was up to his waist when a small boat came along and the operator of the boat asked him to get in. The man said, "No, I am quite spiritual and I will trust God to save me." The water had risen to his neck when a helicopter hovered overhead and put down a ladder for him to climb to safety. Again, he refused, saying, "I am a spiritual person and will trust God to come and save me." Soon the water passed over the man's head and he drowned. Being a spiritual man, he of course went to heaven, but when he arrived he was hopping mad. He demanded an audience with God, and eventually was shown into God's office. He immediately began complaining, saying, "I am quite spiritual and trusted you to save me when I asked. Why did you not save me?" God said that this puzzled him also, and asked the man his name. God then looked through a large ledger until he found the man's name. After looking at the page for a moment, God said, "Oh yes. You are the guy I sent the boat and helicopter."

In addition to paying attention during our daily activities, we will keep the vision of our goal firmly in mind. We will become single-minded, knowing that all we do and think is leading toward our goal. That does not mean we will wander around day-dreaming all of the time, waiting for our goal to appear. We must, of course, take care of the business at hand. However, we will approach our tasks with a new enthusiasm because we are testing out our theory in the arena of reality, and we know that everything we are doing today is bringing us closer to making our vision a reality. This holds true because we are working with a universal law that, if we do not waiver, will always produce the right results.

You may feel the circumstances of your life are so

unpleasant or overwhelming that it is incredibly difficult to keep your vision alive in the midst of such turmoil. Even those who are not in dire straits sometimes get pulled into the confusion and negativity that seem to surround them, and for awhile completely lose sight of their vision or goals. This is understandable and happens to all of us from time to time. The most important thing to do here, and sometimes the most difficult, is to stick with your morning and evening meditations, regardless of how you feel. Soon you will come to know that yesterday's belief systems placed you in your present situation, and that today's new belief systems will place you in new and desired circumstances. This may be difficult, but is by no means impossible. Remember, you can think anything you want to, and what you are thinking and believing is precisely what is going to happen in your life. We have decided to test this premise, and so we stick with it until we prove whether or not it is true.

Not long ago, a woman called me and said she had attended a workshop I had given. She had made her lists of the people with whom she was angry, and had listed her fears and her faulty belief systems. However, she was unable to find anyone to share her list. I put her in touch with a woman I know, and later in that week, she called and said they had shared. However, she felt I should talk with her personally. We made an appointment and when she arrived, she was indeed a pathetic figure. She was pale and drawn and her clothes were wrinkled and unkempt.

However, as is always the case, I found I was talking with a bright individual with as much potential as anyone. She was, however, certainly depressed, and had fallen prey over the years to seeing herself as the victim of her circumstances. She had accepted the belief that she was less capable than everyone else, and was in fact little while everyone else was big. Of course, her belief systems had been demonstrated in her life over and over again.

We talked for awhile about her faulty belief systems and agreed, although she was far from convinced, that she had identified the problem on paper and had given her fears, and her limited belief systems, over to a universal power and they were now gone. All that remained was to replace them with the aspirations she wanted to see produced in her life. She felt that this idea was just too simple to resolve her long-standing fears. She had been unable to seek work for several years and was existing on a small government income. However, she wanted to change and that is all it ever takes. She did not want to remain lonely, insecure,and afraid.

I asked her, now that she knew what she did not want, and had identified on paper the belief systems that had led to her having what she did not want, and had released those negative belief systems; what did she want? She said she had once done secretarial work, could type rapidly, and wanted to do that type of work again. To some of us that may not seem like a very difficult goal; to this woman, it was a goal so far beyond her reach she could not even imagine realizing it.

Often, in this type of situation I have one or two leads I can give someone, but at that particular time I knew of no one who was looking for a secretary. However, knowing that the law of cause and effect works, I had her write down her "right now" beliefs about the universal mind, and together we incorporated her goal into a written treatment. She agreed to read the treatment every morning and evening. I also gave her the names and phone numbers of some people I felt would be supportive. She left and I did not hear from her again.

Several months later I happened to be in one of those wondrous inventions of the modern era, the shopping mall, and I saw her again. Rather, she noticed me and came up to speak, for I would not have recognized her. Before me stood a neat, competent, confident individual, radiating good cheer and the joy of life.

I asked her what she had done, and she informed me that she had simply done that which she had agreed to do. She said she had begun, almost at once, feeling uncomfortable about her surroundings and herself. So she fixed them up, made her home clean and comfortable, and made herself, as she put it, presentable. She said many times she felt lonely and fearful, and she would feel her circumstances were overwhelming. In spite of her doubts, she continued to do the things she had agreed to. She called some of the numbers I had given her, and the people were indeed supportive. But the real change began to take place within her, almost without her realizing it, so long had been her habit of feeling down and depressed. She summoned enough nerve to answer a job advertisement in the paper, but was not hired. This discouraged her, but it also gave her the confidence to answer another. On the fourth try, to her amazement, she was hired. And, again to her amazement, she did extremely well in her new job. She said at first she had been assailed by fear and trepidation, but had been able to stay with her vision, trust her inner power, and test the law of cause and effect until it was proven in her life. What appeared to be a miracle was wrought by applying the principles of life in a positive rather than a negative way, and sticking to them until the desired change came about.

Another example comes to mind that shows how changing belief systems, followed by proper action, always gets results. A highly successful man I know came across the philosophy when he was down and out. He knew the type of career he was interested in, but could not seem to acquire even an entry level position. So he wrote out his goals and worked with his belief systems until he knew for sure he was going to get the right position. He sat in his house every day meditating on his goals, feeling much better; but he did not have any position at all, much less the one he desired, and his finances were running out. He was not willing to give up his vision and take a lesser position, but he realized he must take some kind of action. He had been waiting for some intuitive thought from the universal mind, but nothing seemed to be forthcoming. He began getting the feeling that nothing was happening; that this "stuff" did not work. Finally, feeling he had to do something, he got in his automobile and drove to the very center of the large city in which he resided. He parked and went into a cafeteria for a cup of coffee, still wondering what he ought to do. Should he give up on his goal and just find another job?

While sitting there, he began to overhear a couple of men talking about a new position being created where they worked. As he listened, it dawned on him that this was just the type of thing he was looking for. He approached the men and asked where he could apply for the job. They told him right across the street in one of the large governmental buildings. He went immediately to the personnel department, filled out an application, and without delay, was interviewed. The interview went so well that much of the red tape was foregone; and in a few days, he found himself starting a career which was the exact counterpart to the one he had written down and had been meditating on. The man has since gone on to be highly successful and respected in his field of endeavor.

Before we leave this section on taking action, we need to discuss a couple of additional ideas. We have seen that once we are clear as to what we desire, we will be guided and directed toward that desire, and it will be expressed in our lives. And if we do not feel strong in our belief all of the time, we should not become discouraged or castigate ourselves, but continue to work on our meditation and look and listen for the proper action to take. If we will do this, it will be ours.

However, too often we become discouraged and give up just at the time things are about to turn in our favor. We are like the man who planted seeds, expecting them to produce the desired plants. But instead of letting that process take place, he dug up the seeds every few days to see whether or not they were really growing, finally throwing them away because he could not yet see the plant.

We want to avoid this kind of thinking. Once we have written our goals, we have already prepared the soil by ridding ourselves of limited belief systems. We then water and nourish the soil in which the seed resides, by meditation, by following the direction of our intuitive thoughts, and by following the indications we see and hear in our world. If we continue to do this, the seed must bear fruit. No other thing can happen. However, if we keep changing our mind, or become discouraged and let the soil grow up in weeds of negativity and doubt, destroying the seeds we have planted, we will, of course, not see the desired results produced.

One way to avoid the above mentioned problem is to remember that we have taken the position that we are part and parcel of the universal mind, which, in conjunction with the universal law of cause and effect, always produces results. We are now testing that idea in a specific manner. We have decided that we are individual expressions of the universal mind, and therefore, we can communicate with it. That is how we get intuitive thoughts. We become quite in our meditation and at other times during the day, and simply ask for guidance and direction. Ideas will begin to appear and we will follow those ideas, knowing that they are coming from the universal mind. Therefore, we are no longer alone in our endeavor. By contacting the universal mind from the beginning and throughout our treatment work, we formulate ideas that are much more unlimited than when we were using only our own conscious mind. We find that we are dealing with something that has all knowledge, all power, and is ever creating on the largest scale we can imagine. Therefore, our use of the laws of cause and effect are now directed towards specific results, and all of the power in the universe is producing those results. We simply trust this new position we have taken, regardless of old ideas that make us skeptical, and regardless of our present circumstances. When we do this, the desired results begin to be produced in our lives, and we then know that we are in fact, connected with, and able to use a power much greater than ourselves. Then life becomes really exciting, because we have discovered a universal truth which allows us to have it all. In other words, knowledge of, and contact with, universal mind, allows us to stick to our new position until it is proven in our lives.

A final word about taking action, the law of growth, and our present circumstances. It is obvious that we wish to change or improve certain circumstances in our lives or we would not be involved in this process in the first place. However, some of the circumstances may appear quite negative to us, and we feel the need for immediate and radical change in those areas. Other life situations may appear to be going well and we would like these areas to expand and grow. Whatever the case, we need to get as right as possible with where we are right now. Unless we can do this, it will be most difficult to move out of our present situation to where we want to be. As long as we hate something, or feel something or someone is depressing us and making us unhappy, we give those things or persons power to immobilize us. If we find this happening to us, we must change our attitudes before we can move forward, Our inventory process can help us here.

During a period in my life when I was down and out financially, I obtained a position as an orderly in a nursing home. I was responsible for approximately eight stroke victims who were paralyzed, had lost most of their power of speech, and who had diarrhea every morning. My job was to clean them up and get them ready for the day. At first I hated it. I felt that this might possibly be one of the worst jobs in the country. On my days off I continually applied for positions in my own field, but nothing was forthcoming. I became more and more unhappy and disgruntled. Then, one morning I was cleaning up a fellow named Sam and was talking to another orderly at the same time. I happened to notice that Sam was smiling at me and trying to say something. I bent close to him and finally figured out that he was saying, "You are a nice man." All of a sudden it dawned on me. These were living, breathing, feeling human beings with whom I was working. They were confined to this nursing home, while I was free to go and do as I pleased. Right then I stopped feeling sorry for myself and began making every effort to communicate with and get to know the patients entrusted to my care. Before long, Sam, some of the others, and I became good friends. I enjoyed going to work and seeing them. The work was no longer drudgery, and not long after that I was hired in a very good position in my own field. Although I was quite pleased with my new position, I was saddened to leave my friends at the nursing home, and went back to see them often.

I am not advocating a Pollyanna attitude of light and sweetness for every situation in which we may find ourselves. There have been other times when I have had to take a hard line position, so to speak, and say this will not do. It was necessary to take a stand and change the way things were. However, before making a change, it is important to evaluate the situation clearly and objectively, making sure that all positive possibilities have been explored.

Most of the time, if we look closely and objectively at a given situation, we will find that it is not the circumstances in which we find ourselves that are causing us problems and holding us back, but rather our attitude toward the circumstances. Often we react to our environment without really evaluating the situation. We must not let others tell us, nor can we allow old ideas and habitual feelings lead us to believe we are the victims of our circumstances. We have become actors instead of reactors. We know that unpleasant situations are only temporary. As soon as we begin to realize that our new goals are forthcoming, and begin to know that we are individuals in tune with the universal mind, we rise above circumstances. We know the proper action to take, and in doing so, our conditions will automatically change in accordance with our desires. When we get right with ourselves and our present surroundings, we will be much more able to move in the desired direction.

ENJOYING THE PROCESS

Now that we have written our goals and know within ourselves that they will be produced, and are taking the appropriate action, we want to avoid a common pitfall. We do not wat to fall into the trap of thinking that only the realization of the goals will make us happy, and that we cannot be happy until we reach our goals. If we do that, not only will it be much more difficult to see our goals realized, it will also not be much fun. We want to avoid thinking of this as a heavy or tedious process. What we can know for sure is that if we do not enjoy the process, we will not enjoy the goal.

We should begin, when writing our goals, by thinking of our goals as beginnings, rather than ends in themselves. Often we think, if we had the right job, or the right amount of money, or the right relationship, we would be happy. This usually proves not to be the case. The goal will certainly enhance our happiness, but it will not cause us to be happy. The happy state of mind must begin now, remain with us to the realization of our goal, and continue after we have reached our goal. Thus, when writing a goal, we need to ask ourselves—What is going to happen after I reach this particular goal? How will it enrich my life and the lives of others in an ongoing manner? When I get the house of my dreams, what is going to happen there? Who am I going to share it with? Will it be a place of happiness, joy and love? When I get the woman or man of my dreams, what am I going to do with them? Will our relationship be an ongoing, exciting partnership? Will our love continue to grow? Am I talking about a lifetime commitment, or at this time would I rather have a more casual relationship? We need to be able to answer these questions so that we do not end up realizing a goal which is different than what we thought it was going to be.

If we consider our goals as beginnings, rather than ends we must reach before we can be happy, not only will the attainment of our goals be more satisfying, but the process leading to the goal will be infinitely more enjoyable. Because, if we are beginning to really believe this philosophy, we know for sure that our goals will be realized, in fact they are already ours.

Therefore, the way we feel on the way to getting our goal is the same way we will feel soon afterwards. Thus, if we are miserable on the day before getting our goal, even though our receiving the goal will give us a temporary uplift, we will soon be miserable again.

Today is a stepping stone towards the realization of our goals. That, in and of itself, makes the undesirable situations in our lives much more bearable. We know they are only temporary and will soon change, not for the better, but for the best. This allows us to look much more objectively at our present conditions and to evaluate immediate changes that need to be made. We simply know that we are no longer caught up in, nor are we at the mercy of present conditions. Our goals are real for us now, and they will very soon be an actuality in our life. With this knowledge, the pressure and stress of present conditions begins to lessen. Our minds are on our goals, we feel them to be a part of us, therefore, the present situation is only temporary and not nearly as significant as we once thought. This does not mean we will not give our best to our job, or our present relationships, but that we will approach them in a different manner. Our attitude will be one of expectancy, as we know things are changing for us through the laws of cause and effect. We are no longer at the mercy of people, places, or things, but are in the process of creating a new world for ourselves.

Sometimes, old feelings, negative feelings from habitual thought patterns, will arise and we become temporarily confused or discouraged. The present situation once again seems impenetrable and overwhelming. We get caught up in circumstances that appear negative. Fear, anger, worry seem to take over and we feel as though we are once again losing out. We may catch a cold or become physically ill in some other way. This compounds our fears. Our tendency at this point may be to panic, forget our goals, and try to hold on to what we have, or we may become despondent. This is the time to get stern with ourselves. Not to blame ourselves for something that happens to us all, but to remind ourselves that we have taken the position that we are at one with all of the power of universal mind, and that our belief systems will produce the right results through the laws of cause and effect, and stay with our morning and evening meditations on our goals. Particularly do we need a feeling of closeness with the universal mind at these times. Even if we do not feel like it, and our belief seems weak, we will continue to communicate our desires to the universal mind. This is also a good time to use support systems, a subject we will discuss later in the book. If we will do these simple things, the feelings of despondency and fear will soon leave us and we will once more know we are on the right track, and we will begin to truly enjoy life.

While working toward our larger goals, we also need to begin doing some things that we enjoy right now. These activities need not be directly involved with the larger goals. These are the short term goals, that will do as much as anything, to maintain our happy state of mind and the enjoyment of our life right now. We need to make a list of the things we like to do. What is it today that makes us happy, relaxes us, and aids in our maintenance of peace of mind?

You know what it is you like to do. And make sure it is what you like to do—not what someone else likes. For instance, I am a detective novel fan. I read two or three a week. I do not like the ones with a lot of violence, but rather the simple straightforward upbeat mysteries where the guy gets the girl in the end. This activity gives me a great deal of pleasure. It stops my head from spinning. It relaxes me, and it's fun. Therefore, everynight before retiring, I read a mystery for an hour or so. No matter what happens during my day, I always have something fun to look forward to. My wife does the same with her novels and her music. It makes no difference what the activity is, as long as you have something that daily gives you enjoyment.

On the other hand, if you are involved in activities that depress or bring you down, you may need to take a look at them. Make sure you can afford what you watch on the television, what you hear on the radio, and what you discuss at coffee break. If it is your habit to read the newspaper every evening, or listen to the late news, you are receiving a great deal of negative input. The newspeople are not interested in reporting the one million and one great things that are happening to individuals in our country every day. That is not their job, nor I suppose, should it be. I am not suggesting you should disregard what is going on in our world at large, but you might want to temper your news reports with listening to music that really inspires you, or reading a good book. There is no law against watching the news every other night, or once a week, for that matter.

In addition to the daily enjoyment of life, which may include good books, music that makes us feel good, interesting and positive conversation, and a million and one other things that keep people up instead of down, it is also an excellent practice to plan something every week that is out of the ordinary and really gets us excited. These are also short-term goals that we need to think about, write down, and then do. If we had relatives visiting, we would make an attempt to entertain them. Let's begin by treating ourselves as well as we would our relatives and entertain ourselves once a week. Again, it should be something we really love doing, not what we think we should be doing, or something that someone else loves. Again, it may be a play, a ball game, a dance, entertaining friends, a workshop, a motivational lecture, an amorous evening, dinner at the Ritz. It makes no difference, as long as it is a real treat for us as individuals.

We need these short-term exciting events taking place in our lives regularly if we are to enjoy our lives beginning right now, and if we are going to continue enjoying the process which will invariably lead toward our larger and more significant goals.

CHAPTER VIII
SUPPORT SYSTEMS

SUPPORTING OURSELVES

If we have been conscientious in doing our homework, so to speak, we will have begun to have a new attitude toward ourselves, toward others, and toward the world around us. Not only will some facets of our changing belief systems be new to us, they will be dissimilar to the attitudes and beliefs of most of the people around us. We are no longer giving lip service to the power of positive thinking, we are beginning to live and experience it. To maintain this new attitude, not allowing old habitual thought patterns to intrude, we need first to support ourselves, and second, to receive support from others.

It never ceases to amaze me how badly we sometimes treat ourselves. I am sure we would not treat our friends in a similar manner. We continually talk to ourselves, and what we say is often quite negative. These words we speak to ourselves have more impact on the way we feel, and on the way our lives are going than anything we might be saying to other people. If we are thinking, and we always are, then we are continually saying things about how we feel about ourselves and our world. What is it then, that you and I are saying to ourselves; and what effect is that having upon us?

If we listen to ourselves, we may find out that we are not supporting ourselves very well. How many times a day do we tell ourselves, I cannot do that, I'm afraid this will work out badly for me, certain kinds of people or situations make me nervous. Or we say to ourselves, and sometimes to others, I am tired, I am bored, I am sick, I do not do that kind of job very well, driving on the freeway always gives me a headache, I get so angry when John does that, Mary always makes me feel inferior. Finally, we may be saying, I never have enough money, time, energy, fun. The list could go on and on. So, on the one hand, we have gotten rid of negative belief systems, and have written down our goals with the expectation of seeing them produced in our lives; and on the other hand, we are sabotaging the process by talking to ourselves in terms that do not support us. In fact, much of what we may be saying to ourselves negates the very way we want to be and feel.

Another non-supportive way of talking to, and about ourselves comes from the old notion of not wanting to be conceited. We discount the support we might be giving ourselves. We say things like, Oh, that was nothing, anyone could have done that job, this is just an old dress I picked up on sale, I know he or she is just saying I am pretty, or intelligent, or a lovely person, just to make me feel better.

We need to listen to what we are saying to ourselves throughout the day, and if we find it is non-supportive, we can change it. All of the above-mentioned thoughts and words are the result of habit. And habit can be changed. We have made our lists concerning the negative and limited belief systems about ourselves and have gotten rid of them. However, old habitual patterns of thinking must now be replaced with a new kind of thinking that will support our new belief systems.

We can change habitual thinking by writing down a character sketch of the way we would like to be, and incorporate it into the five-step goal-getting procedure we discussed in Chapter VI.

We begin by saying we are part of the universal mind, thus we are the same as the elements contained in universal mind, and they are contained in us. What are those elements? They are beauty, love, self-confidence, health, abundance, and any other positive qualities we wish to express more fully. Therefore, our statement says I am beautiful, energetic, happy, confident, loving, successful, and so on.

When we have written that down, we need to see if the statement corresponds with what we really believe about ourselves today. If it does not, it is because our habitual thinking has not yet come into line with our new belief systems. So, we begin to change the old habits by saying new and different things to ourselves. A good thing to do at this point is for us to go and look into the mirror. Do we love the person looking back? Are we willing to support that person in his or her every endeavor throughout the day? Do we think that is a beautiful, happy, self-confident, loving individual looking back at us from the mirror? If we do not feel good about ourselves, we cannot feel good about others, nor can we expect others to feel good about us. So we tell our image in the mirror: "Hey, I love you, I think you are great. You are a beautiful creation. You are my best friend and I am going to treat you with love and respect all of the time." This may feel awkward or embarrassing at first, but if we do it every day, we find ourselves becoming more at ease and getting to know and love ourselves. Then, throughout the day, we look at our list of positive endowments, knowing that they are the real truth about ourselves. We also listen to what we are telling ourselves, and when that is not in line with our new image, we change those thoughts to match what we now believe to be true about ourselves. Either thoughts become things or they do not; and if they do, as we know they do, then we will always become the kind of person we think we are. Thus, when we change our habitual thinking about ourselves we will automatically change, and our world will change in its response to us.

If, when looking into the mirror we find ourselves saying, "You are too fat," or other nonflattering comments about ourselves, we need to look at the words we are using and consider the facts. First, are we really our own best friend? To how many of our friends do we say, "You are too fat?" Would it not be better to say to the image in the mirror, "You weigh more than you would like to, and you can change that." The image in the mirror may say back, "I have tried to diet many times to no avail." Then we can remind the image in the mirror that this is old habitual thinking, based on old belief systems that no longer apply. The fact as it now stands, we remind our image, is that we weigh more than we would like to. The fact is also that if one person can lose weight, then anyone can do so. We are not talking about changing the color of our eyes, although that is even possible in our age of technology. We are talking about a normal bodily process, taking in more calories than we burn.

We might then ask the image in the mirror, "Would you really like to be slim, trim, and beautiful?" The image may answer back, "Yes, but I also love to eat." Well, which do you want more, we may ask. It also has to do with health and feeling better. If we find we are undecided we say fine, we will talk about it again tomorrow and we forget about it until tomorrow. We do not go through our day feeling guilty over the food we eat. We do not talk to ourselves, or to others, about the difficulty of losing weight. We simply let it go each day until we decide we really do want to lose some weight. Then we write down how we will look and feel when we lose weight, and we begin seeing ourselves as a thin, energetic, vivacious person. We talk thin to our image every morning. Along with all the friendly, loving things we say to ourselves in the mirror, we also say to our mirror, "You are thin, slim, and just right." We tell ourselves we are that way because it is important to our self-image and our feeling of health and energy. Throughout the day, several times a day, we read and repeat our new ideas concerning our perfect weight. We will soon find ourselves less hungry, more energetic, liking ourselves better, and losing weight.

The same procedure applies to anything we want to change about ourselves. We make those changes by, first listing and getting rid of our negative belief systems in that area, writing out how we want it to be starting now, and changing our habitual thinking in the manner described above.

SUPPORT FROM OTHERS

As we begin treating ourselves as we would treat our best friend, along with knowing that we are not alone and that we are constantly in contact with the universal mind, our feelings of self-confidence and well-being will continue to increase. At the same time, our relationships with others will improve, and we will begin to attract supportive people to ourselves. This brings us to the second facet of supporting ourselves—building an outside support group.

We all need friends. And some of these friends should be on the same path that we are on, supportive of our way of thinking. There is only one way to attract supportive friends, and that is to begin thinking friendship and being friendly. These statements may seem so simple that they insult our intelligence. Yet, many of us say, I have many acquaintances but no true friends. I have no one I can really confide in, no one who I can really trust to share my innermost feelings. That is why so many of us go to counselors. We are looking for someone who cares, and who we can trust. As soon as we begin to really care about ourselves, and trust ourselves and the universal mind, and the laws of cause and effect, we will be able to attract all of the supporting friendships we could possibly desire.

Having become our own best friend, we need to go out into the world and develop our support systems. However, our acquaintances may not understand the philosophy of life that we are now testing. Where can we find positive, understanding friends who will support our endeavors? One of the best places to begin may be a "new thought" church. Churches of Religious Science, Unity Churches, Churches of Divine Science have philosophies quite similar to those discussed in this book. These types of churches are interdenominational, tend to shy away from religious dogma, and talk mainly about how to apply spiritual principles to better one's life. If you are located in a city of any size, there will be several of these churches in your area. If your community is small, they may well have study groups within your area. If not, you can start your own study group. In fact, even if you already belong to one of these organizations, you need to have a regular support or study group. Even if it begins with only two or three people, it will add immeasurably to your personal growth, and to the realization of your goals. Some of us may feel we are too shy to approach anyone to join us in our endeavor. However, if we begin saying the proper things to ourselves, the laws of cause and effect cannot but attract positive people to us, and at that time we must go ahead and risk, asking for what we want. We will be surprised, if we do risk, that there are more people than we realized on our same path. More often than not, we will find them quite amenable to spending one evening a week studying these principles. Once we get over our initial nervousness, we find it is a great deal of fun seeking and finding kindred spirits.

In addition to new thought churches, there are many different self-help programs, lectures, seminars, and classes in almost every community, no matter how small. Check your newspaper, your local schools, and civic organizations for these kinds of activities. If you want a support group, you will find one that meets your needs, no matter where you live. There are more and more people, in every city and hamlet, applying similar principles to these we are discussing, and improving their lives by leaps and bounds.

Some of the activities cost money. Sometimes we

would like to attend a particular class or lecture, but feel we cannot afford it. We would like to buy a particular book or tape, but hesitate to spend the money. Yet, each one of us considers toothpaste, shaving cream, cosmetics, haircuts, and nice clothes as necessities. We spend hundreds, or even thousands of dollars on the outside self. How much are we willing to spend on the inside self? Thousands to improve our looks; how much to improve our minds?

However we do it, we must begin supporting ourselves and creating support from others if we are to realize our goals and enjoy our lives. We will approach this endeavor, not as little people needing support from big people, but as equals who will be giving as much support to others as we will be receiving from them. We are now able to help ourselves, thus we can also effectively help others. This is important for us to know. Life is a give and take process. You always have something to give another, and so does he or she have something to give you. This is one of the wonderful things about life.

I used to think that helping another worked in the following manner. It was as if there was a fire escape extended over an alleyway. If I needed help, the person helping me was perched on the top of the fire escape and would throw a rope down to me in the alley. Then the person would pull me up to his or her level. If I was the helper, then I was the one doing the pulling. If anyone has ever tried to pull someone up by means of using a rope, they will know it is practically impossible. I discovered that to really be of service to another, I need to extend the fire escape down into the alley. However, I then began to try to push people up the ladder and soon found that almost as difficult as pulling. Finally, I realized the only way we can help each other is if I put my arm around you, and you put your arm around me, and we walk up the steps together. Thus, as we go about developing our support groups, we will find that we are giving and receiving in equal parts and everyone benefits.

SOCIAL CONSCIOUSNESS

As we move out into our world with the intention of supporting ourselves and seeking the support of others with similar belief systems, we must also be aware that most of our neighbors, co-workers, and acquaintances are not on our same path. Most people feel that they are pretty much under the control of the circumstances in which they find themselves. The idea that by changing your thinking you can change your circumstances is quite foreign to them; that anyone can feel precisely the way he or she wants to feel, physically and emotionally, simply by changing habitual thought patterns is just too far fetched for them.

When most people in a given society believe a certain idea to be true, they formulate a group or communal belief system. This social belief system, or social consciousness, produces results on a group or community level in the same manner that individual belief systems produce results for the individual. The general attitudes of a given family constellation, company, city, state, or nation, are continually creating results which are the exact replica of the dominant attitude. The impetus usually begins with one or more strong personalities thinking and talking in a certain way; the result is then demonstrated in a given set of social or economic conditions. This is precisely how a person like Hitler was able to change the thinking of a whole nation, with the horrible results that followed.

Of course, most social belief systems are not as radical as those that took place in Germany in the late 1930's. Nevertheless, social thinking produces definite results in our lives and we all can be affected in one way or another. Not all of this type of thinking produces limited conditions. In fact, the great strides this country has made economically, socially, and politically come from social consciousness. The democratic ideal, equality of human beings, freedom of the individual, are all social ideas that produce positive results. On the other hand, many social belief systems can be quite limiting. The people "in the know" begin by talking about the inevitability of an economic recession. Soon more and more people become fearful and negative regarding economic conditions. Before very long, we find ourselves in an economic recession. Of course, our leading economists would say that it would be ridiculous to consider the possibility of social belief systems creating a recession. They would point out the facts of the economic conditions preceding the recession, and explain that nothing else could possibly have happened. We, as individuals in business and professions, readily agree with these learned men, and what happens? We begin thinking in terms of limitation. We begin to fear for our business and income. We think we will soon be much worse off financially. Accordingly, since our belief systems produce results in our lives, we soon prove to ourselves and others that the economists were right. The reason we lost our job or our business failed was because of the recession. That certainly takes the responsibility from our shoulders. We feel we should be happy just to hold on to our jobs in times like these. No one could possibly expect us to improve our financial condition until the recession is over.

Yet, if we look around, we see that some individuals are making money hand over fist, right in the middle of the recession. How can that be? Do they not know about the recession? Can they not hear what the economic experts are saying? They must be one of the lucky few. Nevertheless, the fact remains that some individuals are not being affected by present conditions in the same way as the majority.

We find this phenomenon cropping up again and again throughout history. Certain individuals somehow go above and beyond the social belief systems and allow their individual beliefs to be demonstrated, in spite of the apparent surrounding conditions. Christopher Columbus said, I know what most people think, but I know something different. It is risky to go against popular opinion, but I am going to do it anyway. In another age, some people began saying, slavery may appear to be economically sound, but it is not. More than that, it is an unsupportable institution. It does not fit with what this country is all about. Eventually, that belief took hold, and no one in his or her right mind would support slavery today. There are now many people in this country and in the world who are saying, wait a minute, hatred and war are no longer viable options. Peace, love, and cooperation are the only ideas that will work if we are not going to blow up the entire planet.

Now, what does all of this have to do with you and I? Are we to run out and begin attempting to change the world? Not at all. We are going to change as individuals, and when enough of us change our thinking, it will have an impact on society at large. Our main concern here is to become one of the individuals who can, at any given time, rise above the present circumstances and produce whatever it is we want in our lives. We have the basics for doing just that in the preceding chapters of this book.

We want to take a position that our belief systems create for us individually, and as we expand our belief systems, our lives will be expanded, regardless of conditions or the social belief systems that surround us. We want to keep firmly in mind the idea that our own lives need not be circumscribed by what the majority believes. If our family, our company, our society, appear to be creating general limitation, we no longer have to be subject to that limitation. Our individual belief systems, in tune with the infinite universal mind, will produce any condition or feeling we desire, regardless of what the rest of the world is doing. It is all important for us to remember this fact. We have discovered a power by which we can live. We have discovered how to become free of our own limiting belief systems, and in the same way, we are now free of limitations which appear to be placed upon us by group consciousness or negative conditions.

Therefore, as we go into the world armed with a new set of belief systems, and know that they are producing new feelings and conditions in our lives, we will not allow old limiting habit patterns of thought to regain control. Nor will we allow the ideas of others, nor limited appearing conditions, to override or cancel out our knowledge that what we believe to be true, is true for us.

SUPPORTING YOURSELF WHILE DEALING WITH STRESS

If our mind, in conjunction with the universal mind, controls all of our affairs; and if our minds have the power to create emotional and physical health, as well as financial and material success, it then follows that we have tremendous power. With this power, comes responsibility. We are no longer able to blame others for our problems. If we find ourselves in negative circumstances, we now know we attracted these circumstances to ourselves by the way we were thinking and believing. Our responsibility now is to change our thinking and keep it changed. If we can do this, we will find all aspects of our lives changing immeasurably for the better. If we do not keep our thoughts and words concentrated on what we want, then we will continue to receive what we do not want.

Keeping our thoughts directed towards what we want to see expressed in our lives may appear to be difficult at first. Old ways of thinking and of doing things seem to stubbornly reappear. However, if we have done our work properly up to this point, keeping our thinking clear of negativity is not nearly as difficult as it appears. We really can think anything we wish. Our thoughts are under our own control. We decide how we want to think, feel, and act—in that order. If our thinking is right, we will feel right, and our actions that follow will also be right for us. We do not ignore the world around us, but neither are we at its mercy. We go about our daily business knowing the best is already ours. We are friendly, kind, loving towards ourselves and others. We are able to assert ourselves without slipping into negative or limited thinking. We have the power to change our thoughts back to that which is positive and good.

At the same time, we do not have to watch our every thought or take our emotional pulse every two minutes. We stay as calm and relaxed as possible knowing we are on the right path. We need to take care not to get into negative gossip. If we begin talking in a derogatory manner about others, or about the conditions around us, we can expect these thoughts and words to be as creative as the positive ideas we are expressing. A general attitude of well-being, love, and kindness is unbeatable for keeping us on track and allowing us to experience as much good and enjoyment as possible. If we continually work on our own self-improvement, people, places, and things become much less disturbing to us.

We hear a great deal these days about stress, and the management thereof. The modern technological society in which we live appears to abound in stress-creating situations. We seem to live under the threat of everything from muggings in parks to nuclear annihilation. At the same time, we find individuals who are calm, at peace with themselves and the world, and are enjoying the good things of life. What are they doing, and what can we do, to live joyously and free in a stress-filled world? If we wish, we can use the principles in this book and not react to the stress situations in a negative way. We know that those things which appear to be causing us stress can be dealt with effectively by realizing that we are able to live effectively in any circumstances, that our minds created the stress reactions we have felt, and that our minds, in conjunction with the universal mind, are no longer reacting in the same old way. As soon as we begin to think and believe peaceful, harmonious thoughts, we will begin to feel peace and harmony, and our world will automatically reflect those thoughts and feelings.

There was a time when my life was filled with incredible stress. I was working in a clinic twelve to fourteen hours a day, was on a 24-hour pager, drove fifty miles round-trip on crowded freeways every day, was responsible for fifty patients and thirty employees, and I was going crazy. It was not too long before I became nervous, irritable, and physically ill. Then, due to my wife's insistence, I took a week of vacation. The first vacation I had taken in five years. During that week, I had a chance to sit down and look at my situation on paper. I saw clearly that I had not been taking care of myself physically, mentally, or emotionally. I was not only exhausted, but I had come to believe that the clinic could not survive without me. At the end of that week, I simply handed in my resignation, giving thirty days' notice.

Now, almost immediately, an amazing thing began to happen. I felt good, both physically and emotionally. I was in the same situation for those thirty days, but I was no longer under stress and I no longer reacted in the same way. I cut my hours to eight, stopped browbeating the other employees, started delegating responsibility, and making positive plans for my life. Not only did the clinic not fall apart, but it began to function better. The people who had been giving me the most difficulty became the most cooperative. I began seeing them as human beings and friends. My whole world turned around and the stress was gone. The same situation; except I was using different thinking followed by different action. That was all there was to it. Proof again, that it is never the situation, but our attitude and reaction to the situation that causes stress and discomfort. The clinic is still doing well, and I am a consultant there three afternoons a week. It was time for me to move on to something new.

Moving on to something new also appears to cause us stress. Many people believe that change causes stress. Again, this is not so. Our fear of change causes us stress. We must identify and get rid of this fear in the manner outlined previously. We must do this because change is what life is all about. If we continue to resist change, how will we achieve the excitement and satisfaction out of life that we desire?

I am not suggesting that anyone run out and quit their job. But I am suggesting that we take a good look at our circumstances, see what needs to be changed, and change it. Always, or almost always, the most significant item we discover that needs to be changed is our own attitude. Once we begin to change our attitudes towards our situation, the stress will leave, and miraculously, our situation will change.

SUPPORTING PHYSICAL HEALTH

An area that is directly linked to our mental and emotional health, and vice versa, is our physical health. I make no pretense to be an expert on physical illness or disease. If I become physically ill, I go to a physician. If I have a toothache, I go to a dentist. It is common sense to rely on the skill and expertise of the men and women in our medical profession.

On the other hand, it is our responsibility to keep ourselves as physically fit and healthy as possible. More and more, the medical profession is talking in terms of wellness. Healthy mental attitudes, coupled with proper diet and exercise will go a long way towards keeping one physically healthy. We need to begin with an evaluation of our belief systems about health and wellness. We can look at this area in the same way we would any other belief system. We mentioned earlier that we may be surprised to find that we have some beliefs about being sick, and being well, that we did not realize.

Often, when we are children, we learn some things about being sick. When we get sick, what happens? We get a great deal of attention for one thing. Our parents seem to treat us with more kindness than at other times. Some of us then formulate a subconscious belief system that says when all else fails, we can get love and kind attention by getting sick. Also, we find that we are not expected to do very much when we are sick. We can sort of lay back and let the world and its problems go by. We do not have to feel guilty about our inactivity, because, after all, we are sick. When things are not going as well as we would like, our subconscious may fall back on getting sick so we can get out of the situation and rest for a bit. Finally, there is the idea that everyone gets sick once in awhile. Or, I always get a cold in January, it never fails. If we believe that idea, what happens every January? Our belief system produces a cold. I am not saying that this is the case with everyone or that we should castigate ourselves when we are feeling ill; however, if we will write down our belief systems about sickness and health, and get rid of the old beliefs that seem to tend toward ill health, replacing them with new beliefs of wellness being our natural state, we will find ourselves taking a giant step in the right direction.

If anyone at this time has a serious health problem, by all means they should see the proper medical person and follow their advice. At the same time, if you follow the above procedure and begin to see yourself as well, you will see your recovery take place much more rapidly. There are many books out on health and wellness. I will mention just a few of these in the final chapter. I am also a firm believer in moderate daily exercise, a well balanced diet, and the use of vitamins.

In the final analysis, you are becoming your own best friend. The more you respect, love, and take care of yourself, the more you can give to others and the more you will receive from them. If we are all one within the universal mind, then the way we treat ourselves will be reflected in the way we treat others, and in the way that they treat us. Thus, it is not only important to treat others as you would have them treat you, but, also to treat yourself as you would have others treat you.

CHAPTER IX
SETTING THE PROCESS IN MOTION—AND MAINTAINING IT

Before we come to the end of this chapter, we have a decision to make. Are we going to do the things suggested in this book, or are we going to forget most of it and go on to the next book, tape, or seminar? The reason this book was titled as it was, was not to be humorous but to give the idea that it contains a basic system which, if used, will begin enhancing our lives right now. It is further hoped that the process will not only be started by the reader, but will be continued until definite results are seen. Then each and every new book we read, tape we hear, or seminar we attend, will have a greater impact because we have a basic system for successful living already in place.

There was a time when I read every self-improvement book I could get my hands on. That was a good thing for me to do, except for one problem. I never stayed with one book long enough to do what it suggested. The next self-help book was always going to be the one that had the answer. It would somehow fix me by osmosis, without my doing much of anything except reading the book. Each book I read certainly made me feel better temporarily, as did the lectures and seminars I attended. My life was also gradually getting better. However, it was only after I began formulating the principles expressed in the books into a practical system, and started doing the things suggested, that my life began to change radically and permanently. I was no longer getting a temporary high from hearing a good speaker or reading an uplifting book. I was beginning to build some consistency into my self-improvement program; the end result was feeling very good most of the time, and getting the results I wanted.

There is an interesting and important fact inherent in any uplifting experience that holds true whether we use chemicals, listen to an exciting speaker, or expand our consciousness during meditation. The fact is that when we get temporarily high, we will always come back down to our starting point, or our normal level of functioning. This is so because of the physiological and psychological law of homeostasis, which simply means internal stability or balance. The body and mind will always return to the normal level of functioning for a given individual. It is as if we are standing on the ground and we suddenly leap up the side of a wall covered with vines and grab hold of one of the vines. We are now at a higher level than we were previously, but quite soon we become tired of holding onto our vine and we finally weaken and fall back to ground level until we again gather enough energy, or circumstances force us, to leap again and temporarily grasp another vine. It is what I call the Saturday night bash-Sunday morning crash syndrome; or for some of us the Sunday morning high, Monday morning die system.

The answer to this problem is to stop looking for temporary highs and instead, begin to raise our normal level of functioning. This will be similar to getting a ladder and placing it against the wall and proceeding to climb the ladder, rung by rung to the top. As we move up to each new rung, we are securely and firmly planted there, and that new rung becomes our normal level of functioning until we reach the top. At that time, feeling great becomes a permanent level of functioning, instead of a temporary, once in awhile experience. We can climb this ladder to a higher consciousness and a feeling of general well-being by making a decision to do what is suggested in this book before moving on to the next. Then we need to follow the suggestions of the next book before moving on, thus allowing each set of principles to build on the one before. In this way, our progress will be steady, rapid, and certain.

What is it then that we need to do before moving on? The process described in this book is quite simple actually, and will move us rapidly and securely up our ladder. First we identify anger, fear, worry, and guilt, and get rid of them. That allows our self-esteem, security, ambition, and personal relationships to operate at their fullest potential. Then we identify faulty or limiting belief systems and get rid of them. Finally, we replace the old belief systems with new and unlimited beliefs, and we immediately begin to experience the results of the new and unlimited beliefs in our lives. That is all there is to it. But we must make a decision to take action. This is where the old idea, do it now, comes into play. If we will do this, we will find our efforts rewarded a thousand fold. Instead of O.K., we will begin feeling great, and our lives will become great all of the time, not just once in awhile.

THE PROCESS APPLIED TO CAREER

The idea to keep firmly in mind when we want something to happen in specific areas of our lives is, that what we believe to be true will become reality. This idea follows the reasoning set forth in the earlier chapters of the book. Some of us may still be skeptical. We still are not sure that thoughts become things through laws of cause and effect. We are not convinced that the belief systems we have today are attracting the things that will happen to us tomorrow. We do not quite understand how the law of growth produces specific things from beliefs that originated in our minds. However, the only way we are going to know for sure is to give it a try. A real, whole-hearted, no-holds-barred try. We begin by taking the position that our hypotheis is correct. Belief systems do produce results in our lives. We are now ready to test our new belief systems to gain specific results. We have discussed in earlier chapters how to do this. In fact, you may have already begun this part of the process.

To being with, every human being is equipped with a wealth of talents. You and I have more innate talents than we will ever have time to use. This is an undeniable fact. People who say they have no special talents simply have not looked closely enough. Furthermore, most of our talents, known or unknown, coincide with those things we enjoy doing. These statements may sound obvious, however, the simple and obvious are the things we often overlook. We feel something has to be complicated and sophisticated to be good. We need to go back to basics from time to time.

I have a friend who lives in Nevada. He was a complicated sort of fellow. He made a decent living, but as with many of us, he felt he was not able to live up to his potential. He felt he lacked direction in his life, particularly in the areas of work and money. He would be up for awhile, then down for awhile. One day he came across Maxwell Maltz's excellent book, Psychocybernetics. He read the book, and for once in his life he did not try to complicate or over-analyze the message contained in the book. He simply began immediately doing what the book said, and he continued to follow the instructions in the book until he became one of the top professionals in his field of endeavor. Which, by the way, was a field in which he had no previous experience, and for which he did not know he had a talent.

If we can get it out of our heads that life, work, career, need to be complicated struggles, it will be the biggest favor we can do for ourselves. If we can get rid of that belief system, and change it to the idea that we are supposed to enjoy our work and career, we will be far ahead of the crowd. Because, what we believe to be true about career and work will of necessity become our own reality.

When we are writing down what we want in this area of our lives there are two ways we can go about it. If we are already engaged in the career we want, or if we know what career or business we would like to have, then we write down what we desire in that career or business as if we already have it. If we do not know what career is best for us, we write down what we would love to do eight hours a day, and how much we would like to get paid for it. We write either of these ideas in the manner described in Chapter VI. Then we pay attention to our intuitive thoughts, we pay attention to the world around us, and we take action when the action appears to lead toward our goal. If preparation or study is indicated, we do that also.

I had been working for several years in the field of counseling when I decided I would like to implement a totally holistic approach to treatment. I wanted to give the patients much more responsibility, and set up an atmosphere of self-help right within the clinic. I wanted to set up a structure whereby the patients would begin helping each other, rather than looking to the counselor to fix them, and then bridge the patients directly into self-help groups following discharge. I wanted a spiritual emphasis throughout the process of recovery. All in all, I wanted a great deal. However, the agency in which I was working was not interested in what I wanted. They were interested in what they wanted. I spent some time trying to convince them they ought to want what I wanted. Quite soon, I learned once again a lesson that is sometimes difficult for us to understand. The reason others will not do what we want them to do, is because they are doing precisely what they want to do. And if they think what they are doing is the right thing, no amount of brow-beating on our part is going to get them to change their mind.

Finally, it dawned on me. Why not try out the principles I had been learning? I looked at, and got rid of some limiting belief systems, and then wrote down what kind of clinic I would like to have. I wrote, it would be a genuine one hundred percent holistic health center. It would be concerned with spiritual, emotional, and physical well-being. There would be no holds barred in talking about a universal mind, or a power greater than ourselves. And that the patients would be uniquely involved in treating themselves and others, with the counselors simply orchestrating the process.

The next step appeared to be the sending out of resumes and talking with other clinics in the area. The response was overwhelmingly negative. Everyone, bar none, said you cannot run a clinic in the way described. I was discouraged, but I said to myself, either this stuff works, or it does not. I am going to stay with it until I prove it to be true or false. I was at a meeting a few weeks later when I overheard a conversation about a new clinic starting up in our area. I called the woman whose name had been mentioned as the director. I made an appointment with her and when I explained my ideas, she said they were precisely in line with what she had in mind. Right then and there she asked me if I would like to help write up the new program and then come and run it. I said to myself, what do you know? This thing really works. The clinic was started in an old Salvation Army building; and using the same principles, it grew into a seven million dollar, fifty-one bed holistic health center. One of the finest in the country, and people are getting well there. This example is not an exception, rather, it is the rule. I could go on and on with countless stories of people who knew what they wanted, believed that they already had it, and got the career or the business they wanted.

On the other hand, if we are not in the right career, or if we do not know what career or business would give us the more satisfaction, what do we do? Actually, we do the same thing, in a slightly different manner. We take a look at ourselves and our talents, and we write down what we really love to do with our time and effort. We may not know of a career or business that matches what we have written down. It makes no difference. We need not worry about whether something exists where we can do what we want and get paid handsomely for it. We only need to know what it is that we want to do, and how much we want to be paid. In fact, I believe we should all do this, even if we already have a career or business in mind. We need to know if that career or business matches what we love to do with our time. If not, it may not be the right endeavor for us. We need to begin to think in terms of enjoying ourselves to the fullest, as well as using our talents to their utmost capacity, when we think of work or career.

When I decided to determine what I wanted to do with my time, I discovered that I loved to read, I loved to travel and meet people, I wanted a certain amount of independence, and I felt a real need to tell others about the things I had learned, so they could change their lives for the better. I wrote those things down, put them into the law of cause and effect, and in a very short time, that was what I was doing.

The ideas expressed in these examples may appear to be too simplistic, however, remember that we are working with the universal mind and the laws of cause and effect. What one person can do, so can any other person, by using the laws we have been discussing in the proper manner. If one person can use the laws of electricity to light a room, then everyone else can do the same thing. It makes no difference what the present circumstances appear to be, how young or old we are, how much formal education we have, what race or sex we are, we can always use the laws of cause and effect in the same way we can use the laws of electricity or gravity.

After writing down the kind of career you want, making sure that it really excites you, be careful that you do not discuss it indiscriminately. Many with whom we might discuss our goals have a tendency to be skeptical. We may even be a bit skeptical ourselves at first. One of the popular ideas we run into is the notion of competition. People believe there is not enough to go around, that certain fields are just too overcrowded. On the surface, this appears to be true. And yet, in every field, certain individuals continue to rise to the top in spite of the so-called competition and overcrowding. Why is that? It is because those individuals operate out of a different set of belief systems than the general population. They believe in themselves. They know they are in tune with a universal power that provides their every need. They keep their minds firmly focused on their goal, ignoring the negative admonitions of others, and therefore, reap the benefits of their positive beliefs. That is what we must do. We are exploring a new frontier. Competition does not exist for us. We know there is more than enough to go around. We are in tune with universal mind, power, abundance, which knows no limitations. It is the same power that produces planets, stars, and galaxies, and that same power is within us, waiting for us to use and direct it.

Surely, that kind of power can provide us with whatever we need or desire, and just as surely, it knows no competition. Our own belief systems are the things that produce the results in our lives, not what someone or some group would have us believe.

There is also no such thing as too old or too young; yet we hear those terms all of the time. I am too young to make a difference. I am too old to start something new. These are general ideas that individuals have time and again proven to be untrue. Mozart began writing symphonies at the age of eight. Colonel Sanders, of Kentucky Fried Chicken fame, did not conceive of that project until he was over sixty years old, and began with little or no capital. In fact, the idea of "too old" is rapidly declining. When I was approaching the ripe old age of thirty, I began working towards my doctorate. Several people at the university, whom I considered knowledgeable, told me I was too old to begin a project of that magnitude. I believed them and discontinued my studies. Sixteen years later, I reentered a doctoral program, and to date, no one has said anything about my being too old. In fact, a friend of mine, well into his sixties, is just completing his doctorate in a field previously unknown to him. My parents, in their seventies, recently returned from a wilderness expedition.

The point here is that we are working with what we believe to be true, not what someone else tells us is true. And what we believe to be true becomes the experience in our lives right now, not at some far off date. Thus, it matters not how young or old you are, nor how much competition others appear to be engaged in. It only matters that you have decided what it is that you want to do, and then begin believing, feeling, and acting as if you are already doing that thing. If you will do that and keep doing it, in a short time, the career you desire will be yours.

LOVE AND RELATIONSHIPS

One of my favorite stories concerns a little girl who lived in an orphanage. This little girl, it seems was a bit of a problem for the orphanage personnel. She was an overactive child, forever running here and there, and never quite where she was supposed to be. One day the people in charge were once again trying to find her. They finally discovered that she had climbed the fence that surrounded the establishment and had placed something in a tree whose branches overhung the outside walk. In retrieving the item, they discovered it was a plain envelope. The little girl and her envelope were taken to the Headmaster's office. The Headmaster, when he opened the envelope, found a piece of paper on which the little girl had written, "Whoever finds this, I love you."

I do not know what happened to the little girl, but I imagine she grew into a life quite wonderful, because she certainly had the right idea. If we want love, we begin by giving love, first to ourselves and then to others, and finally to the world at large. If we will do that, we will find ourselves with more friends than we know what to do with. We will find our present relationships improving immeasurably, and if we want romantic love or a lifetime partner, we shall have that also.

There are two necessary ingredients in any relationship: honesty and communication. Invariably, when we are having a relationship problems, one of these ingredients is missing. A friend of mine who does a great deal of marital counseling says the most common complaint in the counseling sessions is that one of the spouses refuses to communicate with the other. We often hear people say, he will not talk about what is bothering him, she will not share her feelings. If my wife and I have an argument, and one or both of us goes off and pouts, then for the period we are not talking to each other, we do not have a relationship. We have become two separate people walking around in our own little world. It is only when one of us says something to the other, even if it is only to say, are you sorry?, that we have regained our relationship. I do not mean to say that people need to be incessantly jabbering away at each other to have a relationship. Companionable silence is also a part of being with someone. However, if you have something to say and do not say it, if I am feeling a certain way and keep that feeling hidden, for whatever reason, our relationship is not all it should be.

There came a time in my life when I felt the need for a partner to share my world, to have and to hold, and all the rest of that sort of thing. In other words, I wanted "the one," a romantic love, as well as a lifetime partner. Let me explain here, the reason for using examples from my own experiences. I have no intention of giving you the idea I follow these principles perfectly. However, since I know my own experiences best, it is simpler to describe them when we are talking about putting the process into action.

At any rate, as is the case with many of us, my past experience at romantic involvement had not been particularly successful. In fact, there had been many times when I felt it just was not worth it. I could not seem to connect with the right person. However, I decided to inventory my belief systems about women and love relationships. I discovered some negative ideas, but on the whole I felt that I had a pretty good attitude towards the opposite sex and relationships in general. So what was the problem? Upon closer examination, I found that due to past failures, I did not truly believe that I could ever have a lasting, fulfilling relationship. It also became clear there were people in my life whom I was claiming to love, but I did not always treat them very well. I said to myself, never mind a true love relationship; how was I expressing love towards my friends, children, parents, co-workers, and the man or woman on the street? Not very well, I concluded, particularly for a person who was going around espousing a philosophy of responsible action and love. So, I began treating the people who were already in my life with more love and consideration. And, of course, they responded in kind. I was then able to turn my attention to writing down what I would like to have in a long-term love relationship.

I decided I wanted it all. I wanted romance and fireworks, so to speak, as well as a lifetime partner. So I wrote down that I felt the universal mind and the laws of cause and effect could provide this in my life. I wrote it down in the five-step procedure described earlier in this book. I do not believe we have to be so specific that we put down five feet two, eyes of blue, so I wrote down the basic characteristics that I felt would be compatible with a cantankerous soul like myself. As I remember, I put down physically attractive, intelligent, sense of humor, willing to make a commitment, and so on. I thanked the powers that be, and released the idea to the laws of cause and effect as if it were already happening.

Every morning for the next six months I read over my request and released it to the law of cause and effect. I felt I was testing out the theory in a really big way. This was the most significant step in my life. Thus, from time to time I would find myself in fear and doubt, but I kept on. Then, one day I met a woman and I said, I want someone like her. I continued working with what I had written for another six months, and found an interesting thing happening. My relationships with my friends and family were improving, and I began attracting healthy, attractive women into my life. I also felt myself becoming more mature and less self-centered.

Then, one evening, the woman I had met six months earlier came back into my life. It so happened that she was well acquainted with a friend of mine, so I finagled an introduction. She was dating someone at the time and did not appear all that enamored with my charm and wit. In fact, she has since said she thought me somewhat of a bore. However, something told me, this was the one. So, I asked her out for coffee the next night. She accepted and the coffee date lasted six hours. At the end of that time, I simply told her I felt she was "the one," and that I was talking about a lifetime commitment. She said I was surely insane, and maybe I should consider commitment to one of our very fine mental institutions. She pointed out that we had just met and that she happened to be a sensible and responsible person. Nonetheless, on the following Wednesday, after I had sent her a single rose, (a friend of mine told me a single rose is unbeatably romantic) she called me and said maybe we should go for it. She is now my wife, my love, and my partner, and the very best thing that has ever happened in my life.

The point here is not that I have any special gift, because I certainly do not. I have as much doubt, as much fear, as much confusion as the next person. The point is that anyone can use the principles in this book to conquer loneliness, to have as many friends as he or she wishes, or to find that special person. Anyone can also improve all of their existing relationships, no matter in what condition they now appear, by using the methods described in this book. If we can remember that honesty and open communication are the basic ingredients of any relationship, and we are willing to change a bit and take a risk, we will find that thing called love.

INDIVIDUALIZING THE PROCESS

This is the point where I become really excited. The

reason for this excitement is that I know from personal experience, that this process will work for anyone, and that means it will work for you, regardless of present circumstances.

This book was written to you personally, therefore I hope you will take the system and make it your own. Anything you feel needs to be changed so that it will be more meaningful to you, by all means change it. This is your book and your program for removing any and all blocks between you and your goals.

Another point comes to mind here. Although we have been stressing the identification and getting rid of limited belief systems and their reinforcers, that is only the beginning. Of course it is an important and significant beginning, and you may be feeling that the task appears to be long and difficult, you will be surprised how rapidly the identification process is completed. You will find it is not nearly as difficult as it first appears, in fact it is quite simple, and it will move rapidly once you get started. The most difficult part of any task, including the identification and getting rid of limited belief systems, is the starting. If you will make a decision to give this thing a try, set aside some time, get out pen and paper and begin, you will be amazed at how rapidly the system works. The rewards will be a new attitude toward yourself and the world around you, and you will be ready to receive unlimited good in your life.

This is where the fun begins. You will begin to see your goals quite clearly, if you have not already done so. Your horizons will immediately begin to expand and you will feel that all things are possible. Not only possible but highly probable. In fact, a sure thing. It will also become clear that circumstances no longer control your life, and never did. Your limited belief systems placed you in any of the circumstances you feel are limited, and your new belief systems will take you to the circumstances you want to see demonstrated in your life. As you write down your goals, you know with assurance that they are being produced even as you write them. This is the incredible fact arizing from your new belief systems.

It is as if you were staying at a cabin near a beautiful clear lake. Sometime in the past, people had said you must go and get water from this lake in a coffee cup. While you are getting your water from this lake in a coffee cup you may have, from time to time, known there was a better way, even seen shiny new buckets placed along the path, however, others had said you could not use the buckets and must continue to use the cup. Suddenly, the truth dawns. You put down the cup and pick up two big buckets and draw all of the water you want from the lake. The lake has always contained all of the water anyone could wish, it is only a matter of the size of your container. How big is your bucket?

After removing the limited belief systems, the amount of good that can come to you has become unlimited. The only limits to your goals are those you set yourself. The only real battle you have been having is with your self-imposed limitations, and that battle is over. In addition, there is absolutely no person, no group, nothing, that can stand in the way of you reaching your goals. Nor has there, in reality ever been anything standing in your way.

There is only one power, one set of laws, in the universe. We are either using this power and these laws positively or negatively, in a limited or unlimited fashion. The laws of cause and effect begin in our minds (cause), and result in our circumstances (effect). Therefore, we are no longer concentrating on the effects we see around us, rather we are concentrating on the cause within our own minds. When we set our goals on paper we have created a new cause and since there are no longer any contradictory belief systems within our mind, the effect will be new circumstances created in exact correspondence to our written goals. It can be no other way.

I cannot stress too strongly the miraculous way in which this thing works. Limitation has been removed. All things have become not only possibilities, but realities for you. The larger your goals at this point, the better. Whatever your mind can conceive of today, will be yours tomorrow, that is the great fact we have been talking about throughout this book. You have truly become master of your fate. You have at your fingertips a systematic self actualization program that cannot, and will not fail. The same mind that has taken you where you are today, is ready, willing and able to take you beyond your wildest dreams. If you have rid yourself of limited belief systems, and have written your goals with conviction and purpose, you can expect to reap the beneficial results of those goals forthwith.

As I mentioned earlier, I tend to become quite excited over the results of this process. Particularly when we come to the goal setting and goal getting part of the endeavor. The reason for this is that I have seen it work in my own life, and in the lives of so many others, that I no longer have any doubts at all that it is going to work for you. The system is simple, yet sophisticated, and it is complete within itself. You need only follow the process as outlined previously, adapting it to your own needs, and the sky is literally the limit for you.

For the reader who has reached this point in the book and continues to be skeptical, I can understand your skepticism as well as I can understand the person in whom these ideas have sounded as responsive cord and is anxious to begin. I was a skeptic to end all skeptics. When I first came across these ideas, I felt the whole business was a pollyannish attempt to seduce rational men and women into a false security and a false sense of reality. Everywhere I turned, circumstances appeared to be in control of my life. Everything from nuclear war, through economic recession, to a bad tempered boss seemed to conspire against me. But more than that, the idea that I could change my own circumstances simply by changing my mind was too far out for me to take seriously. It was only when my life became so bad and there was nowhere else to turn that I was willing to try anything, even a system as radical as the one described in this book. Even when I began working with the process and developed it into a complete and workable process, even when I saw startling changes take place in my life I was still plagued by doubts from time to time. However, I was always forced to look at the way my life had been previously and how it had become something new and wonderful, and could find no other explanation than the power of mind and the laws of cause and effect. That remains the case to this day.

A FINAL WORD

This will, of course, not be the last self-help book you will read. However, it is my sincere hope that you will take the methods described in this book and give them a real try. Even if you are the skeptical sort, or if you have tried other self-improvement techniques before, this systematic approach for changing belief systems and creating new conditions from the inside out, may well be the thing needed to turn your life around, or to increase your present good a hundred fold.

The ideas presented in this book are not mine alone. I have simply taken ideas from many sources and attempted to formulate a step-by-step primer, where by we can get busy and begin making positive changes in our lives right now.

We have taken some basic ideas and formulated

them into a system. Now all we need to do is give it a try. We make a grudge list, and then in four columns discover how anger, fear, worry, and guilt have been damaging our self-esteem, security, ambition, and our relationships. We then release the anger, fear, worry and guilt through the power of the universal mind. Having done that, we can identify limited belief systems, which were being reinforced by anger, fear, worry, and guilt, and release them also. That leaves us with a strengthened sense of self-confidence and a freedom to connect with the universal mind within each of us, and to use the laws of cause and effect to demonstrate anything we want in our lives. We write down what we want, using the five steps of recognition, unification, declaration, thanksgiving and release; and we turn this over to the laws of cause and effect, knowing it is already ours. We read our statement of our desire every morning and evening, meditate upon it, and take only the action that seems appropriate, and that action will always lead us to our desired goal. It is an incredibly gratifying process. All we have to do is to begin doing it.

No matter what our present circumstances, the process will work. If we begin and become discouraged from time to time, we will not worry. Old habit patterns take a little time to change. One of the things that will assist us is the reading of helpful material to begin our morning and evening meditations. So, while going through the process described in this book, we can use the help of other minds to keep us on the right track. Many of you will already have a library of self-help and inspiration books. If not, it is a good idea to begin building one. I would like to suggest a few that I consider excellent.

Ernest Holmes, The Science of Mind, (Dodd, Mead & Co.) is certainly a classic. Some of the ideas in this book have come from Ernest Holmes' treatise. Two more books that are considered classics in the self-help field are: Raymond Barker's The Power of Decision (Dodd, Mead & Co.), and Fredrick Bailes, Hidden Power for Human Problems (Prentice Hall). These books are still in print and can be found in new thought or metaphysical book stores. Another favorite of mine is a book written recently by my friend, James Melton. It contains a great deal of practical information and is called, hundreds of helpful books, many that can be found in your local book stores. They can be most helpful if we continue to use the principles in this book and use the others to add to our basic system.

In the workshops I give from time to time, I ask the participants to write down three really big things they want to see demonstrated in their lives. I then tell them that if they will use the principles described in this book, they can expect to have them within the next year. My greatest thrill is to run into one of these people and have them tell me that that is precisely what happened. One woman, however, during a workshop asked me if I could give here a written guarantee that she would have her three desires within the year. At first I said, yes, I would do that, adding: however, you have to do precisely what we have said every day for the next year or until you have demonstrated your desires. She immediately said, "I do not think I want to go to all of that work." Which meant, of course, that she did not really want to have it all as much as she first stated. That is often the case. Therefore, before you start the process, be sure you want the changes enough to give a sustained effort. At the same time, do not imagine that this endeavor is going to be that much hard work. It will not be as hard as maintaining habit patterns that are not working for you. Also the end result of doing the process outlined in this book is not just getting the things you want, but it is also feeling the way you want to feel. Once you know how to change your belief systems and you begin having real success in your life, you also gain peace of mind, joy, a sense of humor, and best of all, love, and more love.

Some of us take quite a long time before we really want to try something different or new. I know I did. I am not quite sure why that is, but I think it might be because we do not believe wonderful things can happen to us, so why try? It is only when we do try that we experience happiness, joy, and success.

As part of what I do, I sometimes find myself in the area of our city called skid row. One cold and blustery night around Christmas time, I was going to my car when a familiar figure appeared out of the snow. It was Eddie, an old friend of mine from days gone by. He was ragged and dirty, shaking and shivering in the cold. He recognized me and he told me he was badly in need of a drink. I asked him to let me get him a room to get out of the cold. He said no, just give him the money so he could get a bottle and he would find somewhere to sleep. I said, you know, Eddie, I have found an answer. I know how you can turn your life around. He said no, just to give him the money. I gave him a few dollars and my card, and asked him to call me when he was in shape to do so. I saw him disappearing down that deserted street and said to myself, there, but for the grace of God, go I.

I do not know if Eddie will ever call me, I hope so. I believe there is an answer for Eddie. I believe there is an answer for everyone. I do not pretend I know the only answer, or that this book is the only way to change one's life for the better. Far from it. there are many more articulate and greater books than the one you have in your hands. It is simple that these ideas have helped me, so I hope they will help you. I wish you the very best, and please, take care of yourself. You are the only you we have.

For information on requesting Dr. Lund to address your organization, and to order this book or cassette tapes write:

Self Help
P.O. Box 31813
Aurora, Colorado 80041